ASK THE BIBLE GEEK®

Ask the Bible Geek®

Answers to Questions from Catholic Teens

MARK HART

SERVANT
BOOKS

PUBLISHED BY ST. ANTHONY MESSENGER PRESS
CINCINNATI, OHIO

Unless otherwise noted, Scripture verses are taken from the Revised Standard Version of the Bible, copyrighted 1946, 1952, 1971 by the Division of Christian Education of the National Council of Churches of Christ in the USA. Used by permission.

Scripture verses marked JB are taken from The Jerusalem Bible, copyright 1966 by Darton, Longman & Todd, Ltd. and Doubleday, a division of Bantum Doubleday Dell Publishing Group, Inc. Reprinted by permission.

Cover design: Alan Furst Inc, Minneapolis, Minn.

LIBRARY OF CONGRESS CATALOGING-IN-PUBLICATION DATA

Hart, Mark, 1973-
  Ask the Bible geek : answers to questions from Catholic teens / Mark Hart.
    p. cm.
  ISBN 1-56955-344-0 (alk. paper)
  1. Catholic Church–Doctrines–Miscellanea. 2. Teenagers–Religious life–Miscellanea. I. Title.
  BX1754.3 .H37 2003
  248.8'3–dc21

                                                                2002154028

ISBN-13: 978-1-56955-344-2
ISBN-10: 1-56955-344-0

Published by Servant Books, an imprint of St. Anthony Messenger Press
28 W. Liberty St.
Cincinnati, OH 45202
www.AmericanCatholic.org

Printed in the United States of America

    06 10 9 8 7 6 5 4

Dedication

To my niece, nephews, and godchildren—
Megan, Michael III, Colin, Ryan, Karsten, and Dominic—
for showing me who God is and where to find Him.

MARK 10:13-16

Acknowledgments

There are so many, in fact too many, people to thank here—not just those who helped form this book but also those who were instrumental in forming me.

First and foremost, Mom and Dad, you have given me more than I could ever repay. Thank you for your example of sacrifice, marriage, and family. I love you.

To my sister and brothers—Chris, Mike, Tom, Bob, and John—I say, you inspire me more than you know. We can never take for granted how fortunate we are to have each other for siblings. We are blessed beyond comprehension.

Thanks to Jim, Lori, Kaia, and Tiffany, the greatest of in-laws. My sister and brothers are better human beings because of each of you. Thank you for loving them and for raising my niece and nephews.

To Frank, Carlos, Sergio, Josh, and M@, the greatest staff this warden could ever ask for, please allow me to say thanks for doing that. You keep me going.

Thanks to Matt Maher. We may not share blood or name, but you are truly my brother.

And Msgr. Dale Fushek, your courage knows no limit; thank you for never allowing popular opinion to dictate the gospel or liturgical life.

Phil Baniewicz, thank you for your example of what a godly husband and father should be. Tell ya' what, "You be Peter, I'll be Paul."

Tom Booth, the only thing that has affected me more than your music is your friendship. Your ministry has prayed me through the darkest nights of the soul.

Thanks to Randy Raus. I hold you in higher esteem than words can express; don't ever change (Raus kids, I hope you realize just how cool your dad is).

Fr. John Gerth (Fr. J), I have come to value your friendship and respect your vocation more than I ever thought possible. Thank you for your *fiat*.

Fr. Jack Spaulding, if it weren't for you I might not even be Catholic today. Thanks for believing in me before I believed in myself.

And thank you, Fr. Jim, Fr. John, Fr. Don, Fr. Rob, Fr. Neil, Fr. Greg, Fr. Fred. Thank you all for your refusal to compromise His truth. I now understand Hebrews 13:7.

Thanks to all of my buddies locally, especially Bret, J.B., Sweet William, Neilski, Doc, Duke, Larry, Lou, Jesse D., Dave P., Jason P., and Blum. Thanks for putting up with me. You guys exemplify unconditional friendship—"Giddy-up!"

And thanks to Cindy, Billie Sue, Terace, Michelle, Mel, Kara, Debbi, and Erika—some of the wonderful women who patiently put up with my being a man.

To the staff of LIFE TEEN International, the finest and purest servant hearts I have met, I want to say it is an honor to work alongside of you. Thank you, Steve, Jim, Beth, Caroline, and Paul (and your families), for the sacrifices you make for so many. You live Proverbs 27:17. And, hey, let's all "find a balance," huh?

Heartfelt thanks goes out to the LIFE TEEN family (teens and adults) around the globe, especially the many friends I've met on my travels. You are the warriors for the faith and the pride of our Father's eye; never forget that the Word is meant to be lived, not merely read. And speaking of travels, this is for Irish and Sorin, the greatest family a single guy could ask for; thanks for always being so excited to see me when I get home, and thanks for all the attention.

To Pope John Paul II—my hero, "John Paul the Great," the greatest and humblest missionary our world has known since St. Paul, though you would never ask for acknowledgment, you deserve it most. God's divine Spirit, moving through your humble spirit, has changed my life forever.

And finally but *most importantly*, to my heavenly Father, who looks through my constant unworthiness and somehow finds worth. You are the air I breathe. I stand in awe of Your dangerous and sacramental wonders. You chose the nails, and it has been through the scars in *my* life that I have found peace, hope, and healing. When I feared that you had abandoned me, You drew closest, and for that, I am Yours for the taking. I pray You give me "work until my life is over, and life until my work is done." I love You, *Abba*.

Contents

The Bible and Catholic Tradition

Christ said "the Word," and the Church began.

Dealing With Life's Temptations and Trials

The high road to heaven has its potholes.

Introduction

Being mindless is easy. How often do you get into your car and forget where you are going, or in the middle of a conversation stop and ask, "What was I saying?" It's easier to watch television than to read a book. It's easier to hit the drive-thru than stop and make dinner. It's easier on a first date to see a movie than go for a walk. Why? Because the second options each require thought and necessitate attention.

Look around yourself right now. Do you see God? He is there. It's unfortunate that we cannot more easily see God in our midst on a daily basis. Stress has become the norm, time is something "we just don't have," and nobody seems to understand our unique position on anything. And in the midst of life's never-ending busy-ness, we *run* through our *walk* with Christ. I have always believed that the greatest gift we can give one another as human beings is to force the next person to think.

God is right beside you right now, in both obvious and not-so-obvious ways. The question needs to change from "Who is God?" or "Where is God?" to *"How* is God?" How is God working in my life today? How is God making His presence known to me? How is God answering my prayers (and He is)? How do I approach God? How do I look for God? How do I trust God with my life?

The first thing I have to do is realize that God is God and I am not. The second thing I have to do is put God's will before my own. The third thing I have to do is trust that God has a plan for me. And the fourth thing I have to do is be open to His call.

The wisest thing I learned during my years in college I heard not in a classroom but over a basket of buffalo wings. A good friend looked at me and said, "Fish swim. Birds fly." Pretty profound, huh? What he meant was that we give glory to God by doing what we are designed to do.

I am realistic, and I know where my talents do and do not rest. I cannot sing in an opera, I cannot solve difficult mathematical equations, and I cannot hit a hundred-mph fastball. I can give glory to God in other ways, though, by utilizing what He has given me to work with.

I am not a scholar; I am just a Bible geek. This book is not intended to explain all the foundational and universal truths of Christianity. It's not meant to be an in-depth explanation of Scripture in our world today. It's a lot simpler than that.

I love to read the Bible. I have a weird sense of humor. I find no greater challenge or joy than to encounter the extraordinary (God) in the ordinary (the world) on a daily basis. The timelessness of God's truth *is contained* within this work, *not* in the words that I have written but in the Word that God Himself inspired so many centuries ago.

I have often said that I could care less whether or not anyone ever read a single word of mine, as long as they read every single word of His. God's Word is power, truth, and joy. God's Word exposes, challenges, convicts, and transforms, cutting through generations in time like a scalpel cuts between flesh and bone (Heb 4:12).

That's what Christ does, and that is what the Incarnation is all about: *inculturation.* God came right into human culture—born into the dirt, the hopelessness, and the sin of the world. Christ is the ultimate Transformer; He is "more than meets the eye." Christ transforms whores into saints and murderers into martyrs. That same Christ can transform our biblical ignorance or illiteracy into wisdom and luminance if we let Him.

If you're looking for the key that will unlock the biblical and theological universe, put this book down. I think you'll need a book that is far weightier (and, uh, more boring). The stories and analogies in this book are not designed to be earth-shatteringly theological, nor am I setting out to answer the greatest questions about Scripture. As I see it, I'm basically here to do two things: to love God and to chew gum. I'm not making anything more out of this book, so neither should you.

On the other hand, if you, like me, are just a sinner on a journey, struggling to make sense out of this world around you, hoping to find some joy, or peace or truth, well then, read on.

And to any future biblical scholars who may be reading this right now, this goes doubly for you. It's not enough to know the *words;* we need to know *the author.* Never forget that the Word of God exists to be lived, not just studied. Every once in a while, close the books and go play with a dog. Rediscover the life-altering joy that comes from simply living in His presence.

I hope that you enjoy this compilation of Bible Geek® messages, but I pray that you will *put this book down* frequently. We can never allow ourselves as children of our heavenly Father to spend more time reading books about Jesus than reading Jesus Himself, uniquely present in His inspired Word. While reading thoughts about God in a book can help us envision the Lord in new ways, nothing can replace the grace we receive by reading about God in *His Book*.

Much like an appetizer, reflections on God's Word are intended merely to whet the appetite. The main course of Scripture and Eucharist are waiting to nourish and fulfill us, to bring life, and to uplift our souls, continually leading us back to His mercy and to His table, the altar where we are forever altered.

The Word of God draws you and me more fully into the sacramental Church, the apostolic tradition, and the incarnational Christ, found most specifically and undeniably in the Holy Eucharist. Dive into the Bible, and allow the Lord to radically transform your life.

Are you a Bible geek?

"Jesus said, 'I am.'" (Jn 8:58).

Mark Hart
Bible Geek®

Getting to Know the Trinity

It's the ultimate Three-for-One deal

Where Is God?
What's God's street address?

The heavens are telling the glory of God; and the firmament proclaims his handiwork.

PSALM 19:1

Situation Explained

Where can we find God? Where does He live? What's the street address? Bet it's nice.

Solution Offered

Ask most people where God lives and they'll say, "Heaven." Ask most people where heaven is, and they'll point up—up to the sky.

So, the question: "Does God live up in the sky?"

The answer: Yes, and no.

While no *one* place can "hold" God the Father, not even the ever-reaching skies, God is in the skies. And at the same time,

He's not. God is everywhere.

Do you ever look up at the sky on a cloudy day, see the sunlight breaking through, and just think, *God?*

I do. Every time I see light breaking through and sprinkling upon the Earth, I'm reminded of God. Some say that thunder is God bowling. Maybe. (I'll bet He's an awesome bowler.) Every time I hear claps of thunder or see bolts of lightning, though, I think of God (Lk 17:24). When I see a rainbow, I think of God and Noah. Whether it's blue skies or gray skies, *God is present.*

Notice that this verse does *not* say that "sunny" skies proclaim God's glory; it merely says "the heavens ... and the firmament [sky]" declare His glory and proclaim His handiwork.

Know what that means? It means that both "good" and "bad" days, both sunny and cloudy days, can *and do* proclaim the glory of God. Regardless of how dark times might seem or how hopeless a certain situation might look, the sun will rise tomorrow. Just as after the Crucifixion, that "darkest" hour, *the Son rose!* And every day the *Son* rises.

Today, look around you, and find God in both good news and bad news, in the obvious and in the hardships. The hardships just might exist as a way to draw our hearts closer to Him.

Salvation Given

The heavens are telling the glory of God; and the firmament proclaims his handiwork.

PSALM 19:1

Remember, on cloudy days, the sun is still there, and so is the *Son,* even though we might not see Him.

Why Is Taking the Lord's Name in Vain Such a Big Deal?

What's in a name?

God has highly exalted him and bestowed on him the name which is above every name, that at the name of Jesus every knee should bow.

PHILIPPIANS 2:9-10

Situation Explained

Have you ever been called a nickname that was less than flattering? Has anyone ever made fun of your family name or of your parents? How did it make you feel? Why is taking the Lord's name in vain *such a big deal*? Why is it listed up there with "Thou shalt not kill"? Well, there's *a lot* to a name in God's eyes.

Solution Offered

Nowadays, when you go to a card shop, there's usually a rack with tons of little prayer cards with names across the top. Each name has a different meaning, like "gentle one," "strong warrior," or "holy friend." In the eyes of God, names aren't just "labels" to tell people apart. Your name is connected to your "essence"; it speaks of *who you are*.

In the Old Testament God changed Abram to Abraham, Jacob to Israel, Sarai to Sara. In the New Testament, Jesus changed Simon's name to Peter, because through God's grace Simon's essence (everything about him) was changed by God.

God's name is important too. It, too, expresses His essence. A few thousand years ago you couldn't even *say* God's name;

you'd be stoned to death. Nowadays, some people can't even make it through a sentence without using the name of the Lord as a swear word.

Some people say, "If God's so big, what does He care if I swear with His name? He's God; He's got other things to worry about."

The answer: God is *that big*. The Creator of all creation is totally perfect and totally holy. Taking His name in vain doesn't make God any less holy, but it does make His *name* less holy in the eyes of the world.

When we who call ourselves Catholic Christians violate this commandment (or allow others to constantly disrespect God by destroying His holy name in front of us), we are not living up to our call as children of God. Why are so many people willing to fight to defend the honor and name of their mom or dad or family but unwilling to stand up for our Father who is in heaven?

Notice that today St. Paul tells us that at the *name* of Jesus, *every* knee must bow. This may not happen on a daily basis down here on earth, but the Bible tells us that one day it will. Let's make it our goal to change the way others speak about our Father. It seems like the very *least* we can do for our Daddy (*Abba*) who has given us so much and done so much for us— and who loves us, forgives us, and will never leave us.

Salvation Given

God has highly exalted him and bestowed on him the name which is above every name, that at the name of Jesus every knee should bow.

PHILIPPIANS 2:9-10

What Is Your Relationship With God Like?
Who's your daddy?

Pray then like this: Our Father who art in heaven, hallowed be thy name.

MATTHEW 6:9

Situation Explained

What is your relationship with God like? Who is He to you? Is He a supreme but cold, faraway being who controls our lives like a puppet-master? Is He sort of a judge who sits on high sending people to hell? Is He a strict disciplinarian who doesn't want us to have any fun?

Solution Offered

Well, the answer is right here in today's verse from Matthew. God is our Father, a dad who wants the best for His children. He loves us enough to forgive us, direct us, and offer us words of wisdom and guidelines to live by (the Commandments), as well as an example (Jesus) and a conscience (the Holy Spirit).

St. Teresa used to say that this verse was so incredible that she often would meditate on it for hours, unable to complete the Lord's Prayer (the Our Father), which follows in the Matthew passage. She had a difficult time comprehending that God, the all-knowing Creator of all, wanted us to love Him and *know* Him as a "daddy."

Some people have a pretty easy time relating to Jesus, or the Holy Spirit, but then have an incredibly difficult time relating to God. Why is that? God is our Father, it says right there in the passage. (Way to go, St. Matthew.)

Some people think that it's *because* God is our Father, and because so many people have somewhat cold or impersonal relationships with their own fathers. This is not to say that people don't have great, respectful, loving friendships with their dads. Rather, it is to say that most people tend to associate their moms with caring, affectionate, outward displays of love and their fathers with hard, disciplined, less affectionate examples of parenthood.

That same feeling was alive and kickin' in Jesus' day. Most men during Jesus' day didn't show affection, which is one of the reasons that Jesus shocked so many people on a daily basis. Jesus was *so* outwardly loving, caring, forgiving, and affirming that people couldn't believe a man would be that way in public, especially to strangers, lepers, and *sinners!*

Jesus wants you to encounter God and go to God as His child, as a little boy or little girl, dying to be picked up and held in His arms. Do it now, today. Say three Our Fathers. And don't just rattle them off as if you're going for the world prayer-sprint record. Take your time. Spend a good few seconds on each and every word. Think about what you're saying.

At the end of the Our Fathers, ask God for greater trust in Him, like a child should have in a parent, and for the courage and the humble discipline it takes to follow Him completely. He won't let you down.

Salvation Given

Pray then like this: Our Father who art in heaven, hallowed be thy name.

MATTHEW 6:9

Dad is spelled the same way backwards and forwards, because God is in the past, present, and future.

Have Your Parents Ever Embarrassed You?
Are you old enough to cross the street alone?

For I, the Lord your God, hold your right hand; it is I who say to you, "Fear not, I will help you."

ISAIAH 41:13

Situation Explained

As a child, were you in a hurry to grow up? Did your parents ever embarrass you? Do or did you ever ask your parents for more freedom, privacy, or responsibility?

Solution Offered

I was sitting at a stoplight the other day and saw a father and his young son (probably about four years old) waiting to cross the street. When the signal changed, the child raised an open hand to his father. The dad then took him by the hand, and they carefully made their way to the other side of the street.

As I watched them, I was reminded of this passage. Here God is saying to Isaiah, "Stick with Me, kid. *Give* Me your hand, and I'll lead you through this sometimes dangerous and difficult world."

Why was Isaiah successful? Isaiah allowed himself to be led by the Lord, instead of trying to do everything on his own (like most of us try to do).

When I was a kid, I always reached for my mom's or my dad's hand before crossing the street. The world was much bigger then. As I grew up, though, I quit reaching for it. In fact, it got to a point in junior high and high school where I was embarrassed of my parents because of the things that they'd say, or the car they drove, or whatever. I would even make Mom drop me off a block or two away from the mall, just so I wouldn't be seen getting out of her minivan (with the wood paneling on the sides).

I feel foolish about that now, especially given how much my parents love me and how many sacrifices they made to put food on our table and clothes on our backs.

It's the same with God, I think. Around junior high and high school, many of us might feel a little awkward about being "seen" with God or even opening our hand(s) to Him, even at church. We forget how much He loves us and the sacrifice He made for us, the greatest sacrifice: being destroyed on a cross so many years ago.

Remember what Jesus tells us in Matthew 10:33, "Who ever denies me before others, I will deny before my heavenly Father."

We should never be ashamed of our parent(s)—including our heavenly Parent. This week let's really allow ourselves to be led by *God*. Let's open our palms when we pray and allow our Father in heaven to take us by the hand and lead us through the dangerous intersections of life.

Salvation Given

For I, the Lord your God, hold your right hand; it is I who say to you, "Fear not, I will help you."

ISAIAH 41:13

Be sure to look both ways before crossing the street; but also remember that God's got us in the palm of His hand.

Heaven Is for Children
Being a brat is not child's play.

Truly, I say to you, whoever does not receive the kingdom of God like a child shall not enter it.

MARK 10:15

Situation Explained

Do you ever feel old? Do you sometimes wish you could go be a kid again, without worries or stress or expectations? Without responsibilities? Things sure were simple as a kid. Jesus says that things can *still* be that simple.

Solution Offered

Let me ask you, "Are you a child of God or a brat of God?"

- A child takes what the parent gives. A brat whines when the item given isn't exactly what he or she wants.
- A child depends on the parent for everything. A brat goes to the parent only when in need.
- A child has manners and says "please" and "thank you." A brat has orders and says "now!" or, "You just don't love me."
- A child does what the parent says. A brat does what he or she wants.
- A child runs to the parents and wants to be with them. A brat waits until called.
- A child is open to help and advice. A brat refuses to accept help or ask for it.
- A child admits being wrong or bad. A brat blames everybody else when in trouble.

Now, these are generalizations, but you get my point.

God tells us that we need to be like children because kids are *obedient* and *dependent*. I think I'm more like a brat most of the time, to be honest. Instead of trusting God and submitting to His will and His Commandments, usually I would rather spend my time looking for loopholes, trying to find ways to cut corners or justify the sins that I commit. Does this sound familiar to any of you?

Start today and try to become more childlike. Have fun, be a little "dorky," and laugh! Make it your goal to view life and the world with the same newness and awe that you did when you were tiny.

Praise and thank God for all of the important people in your life, *even if* some of them drive you crazy. Honor God by being obedient to your parents and more patient with your brothers and sisters. When you look at your family, thank God for them.

God has set aside the kingdom of God for the childlike—for those who are loving enough to trust and obey Him and humble enough to depend on Him.

Salvation Given

Truly, I say to you, whoever does not receive the kingdom of God like a child shall not enter it.

MARK 10:15

Growing *old* is mandatory; growing up is *optional.*

Does God Have Ears?
What does God look like?

Lord, listen to my cry for help! Listen compassionately to my pleading!

PSALM 130:2, JB

Situation Explained

What does God look like? Ever thought about it? I have.

Solution Offered

Whenever I picture God, for some reason I always picture an older guy with a long gray beard, flowing white robes, sandals (probably Birkenstocks), and an hourglass watch strapped to His wrist. Who do you picture?

In the psalm today we hear David begging the Lord to acknowledge him, asking for His ears to hear him and his cry. So here's the question: Does God have ears?

The Book of Genesis tells us that we're made in the image and likeness of God (Gn 1:26), right? So does that mean that God looks like us or that we look like Him?

No, neither one exactly. It means that we are made to respond to God's call. We are created with a "God-shaped" heart, and we are created to be holy.

So does God have ears? No, God does not have ears.

How do I know? Because ears would limit God. Even the perfect ears that God would have would be able to hear only a certain number of prayers, because ears have limits as to what they can "take in." And limits are the one thing that God doesn't have. That's not God.

God is absolutely without limit. There's no limit to His love, power, or mercy. You and I should take great confidence in the fact that God can and does hear all of our prayers, because God is *that* perfect, He is *that* big.

Pray, right now. Pray that we would realize God's presence in our lives and that we'd be more trustful of God, knowing that when we pray, He hears *and* responds to us. And we can hear His response.

Ever thought about that phrase "listen up"? It's not just a phrase but good advice.

We all think heaven's up, right? *So* listen *up!*

Salvation Given

Lord, listen to my cry for help! Listen compassionately to my pleading!

PSALM 130:2, JB

The question isn't whether or not He has ears; it's whether or not we trust that He's listening.

Does Milk Go Bad in Heaven?
Got God?

I will give them a heart to know that I am the Lord; and they shall be my people and I will be their God, for they shall return to me with their whole heart.

JEREMIAH 24:7

Situation Explained

I was in God's kitchen the other day. The place is amazing. It's always stocked with food, everything you love to eat, and you can eat as much as you want and never gain a pound. Another bowl of ice cream? No problem. Large pizza at 3 A.M.? Have at it.

I wanted some cereal, so I poured it into my bowl and opened the fridge to grab the milk.

One problem: There was no expiration date on the carton. Do I drink it?

Solution Offered

"Abba, is this milk OK to drink?" I asked.

"Of course, My son," God replied.

As I sat enjoying my cereal, the question kept rolling

through my head, "Why no expiration date on the milk here in God's kitchen, in heaven?" I finally had to ask.

"Well, BG," God replied, "I don't work on an 'earthly' clock or schedule like you do. I am timeless. I mean, I'm God, and I don't give up easily. In fact, I don't give up at all. Do you understand what I'm getting at?"

It hit me. For me, once the milk goes bad, it can't be good or fresh again, and I throw it out. What if it was like that in my relationship with God? What if once I went "bad" that was it, and God just discarded me? In God's perfection and grace, though, the "milk" can always be "good" again, and I always have a shot. As long as I am living, it's *never* too late for me to return to Him.

If there are people in your life who you feel have "gone bad" and who you've given up hope on—people who you maybe think are "past their expiration date"—don't give up, don't ever give up on them. Pray for them. Pray that in God's perfection they will, as today's scripture says, "return to God with their whole heart." He made them—created them and formed them—and it's in God that they will (someday, hopefully) find true peace.

God: He does the body (mind and soul) good. Very good.

Salvation Given

I will give them a heart to know that I am the Lord; and they shall be my people and I will be their God, for they shall return to me with their whole heart.

JEREMIAH 24:7

Got God?

What's the Only Word That God Doesn't Know?

Let's use His dictionary.

For with God nothing will be impossible.

LUKE 1:37

Situation Explained

"He'll *never* change." "That'll *never* happen." "We'll *never* agree."

Never may be a word for us, but I was reading through God's dictionary the other day (He invited me to His house for a barbecue. Adam was making his famous ribs, Eve made applesauce, and Moses was making "manna-cotti"), and the word *never* isn't in God's dictionary. Why isn't the word *never* in God's dictionary?

Solution Offered

This might be the easiest verse to memorize out of any that we've looked at so far. Memorize this one. Learn it. Know the chapter and verse. This is one that we should *never*—oops, I did it again (sorry, Britney, I stole your line).... What I meant to say is that this verse is one that we should always remember.

I always laugh at how little faith I have. There have been situations in my life when I'd say things like you read above—like, "No matter what happens, they'll *never* change." Sometime later God always seems to knock me off my seat and remind me that I can't ever say that someone will *never* change, because I don't know the will of God, and I can't begin to understand how deep His love and mercy are.

St. Augustine is now known as one of the greatest thinkers and saints of our Church, but he didn't surrender his life to God until well into the middle of his life—and only after years upon years of intense, consistent, and sincere prayer by his mother, Monica (also a saint—well, she had better be after all of that prayer, huh?).

The mere fact that we humans use the word *never* so often just goes to show how little faith we have. But remember what St. Luke's telling us today: "With God nothing will be impossible." That area of your life that you struggle with, don't surrender to it. Keep fighting it, keep trying, keep offering it up in prayer, and someday, with God's help, you will win out.

That person in your life whom you want to give up on—the one who constantly hurts you or themselves, the one who won't listen to you no matter how hard you try—that's the one you need to keep praying for, because through prayer, the will of God will be done in that relationship. This doesn't mean that we should stay in an unhealthy relationship or allow people to continue to hurt us; it means that we need to be big enough people to pray for those who hurt us or make our lives more difficult (Mt 5:44).

Just remember to never, never, never, never, never, never, never, never, never, never, never say never when you're talking about God or dealing with God, because what does Luke tell us in chapter 1, verse 37, everybody?

You got it! I've *never* been prouder. Um, what I, uh, what I mean is that I can't think of a time in which I have been prouder of you.

Salvation Given

For with God nothing will be impossible.

LUKE 1:37

Never underestimate the power to change yourself. (There I go again.)

Ever Felt "Worthless"?
What's your worth?

Lead a life worthy of God, who calls you into his own kingdom and glory.

1 THESSALONIANS 2:12

Situation Explained

Have you ever felt really guilty? Ever felt like God could never forgive you for things you've done? Ever feel like you're not worth His love or the blessings He's bestowed upon you? Yea, I do sometimes, too.

Solution Offered

You know what? I am unworthy to be the Bible Geek®. Very unworthy. I am unworthy to get to write to so many through a book and through e-mails. I am unworthy even to call myself a Catholic Christian some days. I am weak, and I am a sinner.

You know what else? Because of Jesus, my human unworthiness is OK. Because of His resurrection, I have a new hope and a new call. My goal *has* to be His home, His kingdom— heaven. And if heaven isn't our goal, we are in deep trouble.

Sometimes people make the mistake of thinking that because we're unworthy of God's total and unconditional love, and because we are sinners, we are worthless.

That's not true. Just because you and I are unworthy *doesn't mean* that we're worthless.

You and I have a tremendous amount of worth in God's eyes. Sometimes when we sin, though, we start to doubt our worthiness, and that's exactly what the devil wants us to do. We start to doubt our ability to follow God (and say it's too hard), we start to doubt the importance of Church (and say it is boring or pointless), and we start to feel as though God is too disappointed in us to forgive us (and say we're not strong enough).

Remember: "Church is a hospital for sinners, *not* a museum for saints."

Today St. Paul is reminding us that through God's grace, we're all worthy of God and of heaven. And he encourages us to live so as to show God every day just how worthy we really are.

You have more worth than you know. Believe in how much God loves you. Give God permission to love you today. Simply close your eyes and whisper, "Jesus, I give You permission to work in my life."

Are you scared to do it? Do you not want to do it? Consider that a sign of your need to do it that much more. Say it a few times and mean it—I dare you.

Salvation Given

Lead a life worthy of God, who calls you into his own kingdom and glory.

1 Thessalonians 2:12

Live for God. He's *worth* it.

Does God Feel Pain?
Ever watch ER? That's nothing...

They stripped him ... plaiting a crown of thorns they put it on his head,... and kneeling before him they mocked him.... They spat upon him ... and struck him on the head.... and led him away to crucify him.

MATTHEW 27:28-31

Situation Explained

Ever heard the term *excruciating pain?* Do you know where it comes from? The word actually had to be invented. No one had a word to describe a pain as intense as a crucifixion, so a new word was created. The word *excruciating* literally means "out of the cross."

Solution Offered

In today's society it's not always popular to tell the truth. Talking about what "really" happened on that hill two thousand years ago makes people uncomfortable. But Jesus didn't go through what He went through to have it sugarcoated.

What really happened? Read on, if you can take it. Good Friday isn't about what's "comfortable." You don't have to read this, but it couldn't hurt—not like it hurt Him.

- He was so overcome with stress and anxiety that He sweat blood. It's called hematidrosis. Chemicals break down the capillaries in the sweat glands, releasing blood. Ever been *that* stressed?

- He was stripped in public. Can you imagine the humiliation?

- He was whipped and beaten. Each whip, made of braided leather with metal balls and hooks woven into each strap, imbedded in and tore the flesh, up to thirty-nine times from each soldier.

- Thorns were placed upon His head, piercing His scalp. Ever cut your head?

- He was struck on the head by a heavy reed, several times.

- His muscles and nerve endings exposed, every movement sent intense pain throughout His body as the heavy crossbeam was given Him to bear.

- His every movement, every jolt, agitated and reopened His wounds. He couldn't move an inch without feeling the pain. The narrow city streets offered no respite from the jostling of the crowd.

- Suffering from intense dehydration, His kidneys stopped working, and His body could not produce fluids. His heart was racing to pump blood that wasn't there. His blood pressure dropped, making Him collapse and faint. And there wasn't a doctor around.

- He had nine-inch spikes driven through His wrists, piercing the Median nerves. Take the pain of hitting your "funny bone" and multiply it by a thousand.

- His arms were stretched at least six inches, dislocating both of His shoulders. I've dislocated my shoulder—the worst pain I've ever experienced.
- His feet were nailed to the crossbeam, pain shooting throughout His body.
- Raised up by ropes, His flesh tore. Words cannot express ...
- He went into respiratory acidosis—meaning carbon dioxide in the blood was dissolved as carbonic acid, increasing the acidity of the blood and leading to a very irregular, erratic heartbeat.
- Fluid gathered around the heart in the membrane, a condition known as pericardial effusion. Around the lungs, plural effusion caused by the sustained rapid heart rate slowly destroyed the entire internal system.
- His intense blood loss caused Him to go into hypo-volemic shock, basically shutting His body down.
- Unable to lift Himself to breathe anymore, intensely dehydrated, muscles failing, blood pressure falling—He breathed His last, handing over His Spirit, finishing Passover.
- He had a lance (large sword) thrust through His side, piercing His lung.

For Jesus, it wasn't about His own needs or will; it was about His Father's will and the needs of the many (you and me).

For you, right now in your life, this week, *who* is it about? Is it about your will, your needs—or His?

If you answered that it's about you, what would it take for

you to change? What else would God Himself, Jesus Christ, beyond the Crucifixion, need to endure for us to put Him first?

Salvation Given

> *They stripped him ... plaiting a crown of thorns they put it on his head,... and kneeling before him they mocked him.... They spat upon him ... and struck him on the head.... and led him away to crucify him.*

MATTHEW 27:28-31

It's called the Passion because that's *how* He loves you—passionately.

Did Nails Hold Jesus to the Cross?
Let's talk about love.

He died for all that those who live might live no longer for themselves but for him.

2 CORINTHIANS 5:15

Situation Explained

Who is the most important person in your life?

Solution Offered

So, who is it? Who is the most important person in your life, right now, today?

Many of us would respond with the name of a family member, or a boyfriend or girlfriend, or husband or wife. Some would respond with the name of their best friend.

Think hard; I'll wait. Of all of the people in your life today, whom do you care about the most? Who means the most to you? Whose happiness means the most to you?

The sad truth is that as much as we love or care about another person, there are many of us alive today who will find the answer to this question *not* in another but in the *mirror*.

For years my favorite two phrases were "I don't want to" and "because I don't feel like it." I was a very selfish person. Actually, it hurts to say this, but I still am pretty selfish sometimes. As much as I care about others (or claim to), a lot of times I still put my wants and needs ahead of others'—because I feel like it, or it's more comfortable, or it's easier.

What if Jesus had done that instead of hanging on that Cross?

Make no mistake: Nails didn't keep Jesus on that Cross; *love* did.

That person you thought of first, or those people you thought of, when I asked you who is *most* important: Would they *die* for you? Truthfully? Would Jesus? Yes. Did Jesus? Yes. Does that really mean anything to you? Yes.

That's love, true love: to be willing to die for another (see Jn 15:13).

So today's verse is telling us two things:

Real love means sacrifice and death.

If we want to experience true love, we need to put our own needs and wants second to God's.

He has a plan for you. You can follow it, or you can fight it. Your choice.

Just remember, the easy way out is just that—the *easy* way out.

This week have more faith in God. He has faith in you.

Salvation Given

He died for all that those who live might live no longer for themselves but for him.

2 CORINTHIANS 5:15

Anything easy has its cost.

P.S. As a final thought, to quote a classic movie, *The Princess Bride:* "Death cannot stop true love."

That's what Easter *is:* proving that death cannot stop true love.

(Oh, and, by the way, if you've never seen *The Princess Bride*, I highly recommend that you see it. Not to do so would be, well, "inconceivable.")

Where Do Rainbows Come From?
The first houseboat...

This is the sign of the covenant which I make ... for all future generations: I set my bow in the cloud and it shall be a sign of the covenant between me and the earth. When I bring clouds over the earth and the bow is seen in the clouds, I will remember my covenant which is between me and you and every living creature.

GENESIS 9:12-15

Situation Explained

Where do rainbows come from?

Solution Offered

All right, all you amateur meteorologists out there, let's not get overly scientific. Think back to Sunday school: Remember Noah? The guy with the ark? OK, stick with me.

In today's verse, part of the conversation between God and Noah, we see that God gives us the rainbow as a sign of the covenant between Him and Noah. Now, a covenant is pretty serious. It is more serious than any contract. You see, a contract is when you have an exchange of goods and services, like I give you ten bucks and you mow my lawn (which could use it, actually). A covenant, however, is an exchange of *self*, meaning here that Noah pledges his loyalty and obedience to God and God promises, out of love, not to flood the entire earth again.

Why the rainbow? What does the rainbow do besides lead us to fightin' Irish leprechauns' gold?

Well, the rainbow is a beautiful bridge between heaven and earth. Also, it comes after a rain. Now, rain is very interesting: It brings life and death. Rain provides our drink and waters the crops we need for survival, but it can also bring intense flooding, like with Noah.

I like to think of a rainbow as a *"What's up?"* from God. It's like He's using every color we know to say hello, remind us of our covenant with Him, and show us that the rain can't last forever—that sunnier days are just around the corner.

God formed a covenant with you and with me at our baptism, reminding us that He loves us unconditionally and that nothing can separate us from Him. At the same time—through our obedience, love, and faithfulness—we fulfill our half of the covenant with God, putting Him first.

The beauty of the rainbow is that every time the skies get dark and we're faced with a gray and gloomy day, God lets the sunlight peek through the clouds to shine on us. He provides the bridge of light, an array of beautiful colors from heaven to earth.

Sundays are special days for us to focus on and return to Christ. Christ is the rainbow on Sunday after a challenging week, a renewed celebration of that first Easter weekend.

Salvation Given

This is the sign of the covenant which I make ... for all future generations: I set my bow in the cloud and it shall be a sign of the covenant between me and the earth. When I bring clouds over the earth and the bow is seen in the clouds, I will remember my covenant which is between me and you and every living creature.

GENESIS 9:12-15

I used to get depressed by the rain, only to have a rainbow cheer me up.

Only God can make a rainbow. (Sorry, Skittles.)

The Bible and Catholic Tradition

Christ said "the Word," and the Church began.

Ever Feel Like Not Going to Mass?
Mass confusion ... Mass appeal?

For I long to see you, that I may impart to you some spiritual gift to strengthen you, that is, that we may be mutually encouraged by each other's faith, both yours and mine.

ROMANS 1:11-12

Situation Explained

"I don't feel like going to Mass; I don't get anything out of it." "Why do I have to sing?" "I don't have to go to church; I pray better by myself at home."

These are all popular excuses that most of us have either used or heard. Phrases like these point out that, for most people, there is "Mass confusion" (pun intended).

Solution Offered

At some point we've probably all heard the Holy Mass that we celebrate on Sundays also called a (Anyone?... Anyone? ... Bueller?) liturgy.

What's a liturgy? One definition is that it's a *public* work done in the *service* of another. That means that when you and I go to Mass, we're not just going for ourselves, to receive something. We're going for *others*, to *give* something.

Community is so important to the Mass. In fact, community is one of the four places we experience Christ in the Mass as Catholics (the other three being the Eucharist, the Word, and the priest).

St. Paul, in the above verse, is telling the Romans how much he'd like to see them, to pray with them, and to share the Eucharist and the Word with them. He understood the importance of community and the incredible effect that prayer with our brothers and sisters in Christ can have.

Reread this verse, however, and put God in the place of St. Paul. Listen to God's voice and hear what He's telling you and me today. This is an invitation to Mass, to adoration, *to prayer.*

Sometimes, I think, we just figure God isn't watching us, that He's too busy to pay attention to us unless we're talking to Him (and sometimes we doubt it even then). The kicker is that God, since He is timeless, perfect, all-knowing, all-power-ful, and so on, can *never* run out of room or attention for us. His "spiritual switchboard" can *never* overload.

God is the Dad who loves to have His children come home and spend time with Him, come around the table and eat. He isn't the dad who wants to see his kids for only one hour a week or during the holidays.

When's the last time you caught a daily Mass, or went to adoration when you didn't have to or when it wasn't an "organized" prayer time? Find a half hour in your schedule this week, tell no one, and *get there.* Look at the verse below. Dad is *longing* to share something with us and to strengthen us.

Salvation Given

For I long to see you, that I may impart to you some spiritual gift to strengthen you, that is, that we may be mutually encouraged by each other's faith, both yours and mine.

ROMANS 1:11-12

See ya' at the dinner table.

Is Jesus *Truly* Present in the Eucharist?
You are what you eat.

Now as they were eating, Jesus took bread, and blessed, and broke it, and gave it to the disciples and said, "Take, eat; this is my body."

MATTHEW 26:26

Situation Explained

Is Jesus *truly* present in the Eucharist?

Solution Offered

One question: What did Jesus say?

Jesus is coming to *your* Church this Sunday, in the *flesh* ... (just like every Sunday). He's not only asking you to believe, but inviting you to experience heaven on earth. Ya', it defies all logic—God coming to us in simple bread and wine. But then, Jesus defied all logic:

- Jesus came to us, *not* a royal baby on a throne, but a simple child in a manger.
- Jesus lived *not* as a powerful political ruler but as a common carpenter.
- Jesus spread a message *not* of war and conquest but of peace and forgiveness.
- Jesus preached the gospel *not* just through words but also through actions.
- Jesus desired *not* to be served but to serve, washing the feet of the apostles.
- Jesus, the King, wore a crown *not* of gold but of thorns.
- Jesus was elevated *not* in social stature but naked and bloodied upon a cross.

- Jesus was *not* buried with a royal procession but laid in a simple, unmarked tomb.

Jesus comes to us at *every* Mass, *not* with bright lights and a big show but in simple bread and wine. Why? I like to think that it's because *simple* is Jesus' style.

If I were God, I wouldn't choose to come in bread and wine. But thank Him that I'm not He.

Bread and wine: If it's good enough for Jesus, it ought to be good enough for me.

He said it, and I have no reason to doubt Him. He's gotten me this far.

Remember what the great author C.S. Lewis once wrote:

"The command, after all, was, *'Take and eat,'* not *'take and understand.'*" Lord, I don't fully understand it, but I sure do appreciate it.

Salvation Given

Now as they were eating, Jesus took bread, and blessed, and broke it, and gave it to the disciples and said, "Take, eat; this is my body."

MATTHEW 26:26

A few final thoughts:

Whether you struggle with believing in the true Presence of Christ or not, it never hurts to spend some time really thinking about it.

Can the people around you at Mass tell that *you* believe Jesus is truly present? If not, let that be your new goal.

Pray for the faith, this Sunday, to see Jesus in the Eucharist in a new way.

The Eucharist: It's so simple that it's mysterious, and so mysterious that it's simple.

Ever Feel Like God's Not Present in Your Life?
"Hey, Jesus, where are You?"

I am with you always, to the close of the age.

MATTHEW 28:20

Situation Explained

Do you ever doubt that God exists? I mean, do you ever sit there at Mass and just think, "What if all of this is just made up? What if it's all fake? What if I'm going through all of this—trying to live according to what's right—and it's all a big lie?"

If you have, you're like 90 percent of all Christians at one point or another (and the other 10 percent just don't admit it!).

Solution Offered

This verse is the very last sentence in the Gospel of St. Matthew, but it's one of the most important. You see, Matthew was writing to the Jewish people, and for years (thousands of years, actually) the Jews had been waiting for the Messiah. When the Messiah finally came—Jesus, that is—many followed Him and believed, but many didn't. A lot of people had a hard time believing that Jesus was the Messiah, because they thought the Messiah would come out of the sky on a fiery chariot and cause the Romans (who were killing and persecuting Jews) to have, well, a really bad day.

Now, imagine you're an apostle, standing on a mountain. Jesus, whom you've followed and pledged your allegiance and life to, has died and risen. Think about that: He died, and He rose from the dead. But now He's ascending on a cloud right in front of you. He promises He'll never leave you. You gotta be thinkin' that some Cliff Notes would be great right now, because you can't figure out what's going on.

Remember, if Jesus were alive today, walking around in Jerusalem, CNN or someone would report it. So the question arises, *"How* could Jesus be with *all* of us until the end of time?" Yes, by the Holy Spirit, but more directly through the *power* of the Spirit. Yes, you got it: The Eucharist.

Over three hundred thousand times a day in our world, the Holy Mass is celebrated in countless languages and hundreds of countries, with the same exact readings and prayers. As Catholic Christians you are part of something much bigger than yourselves, something with a rich history and a two-thousand-year tradition. On Pentecost we celebrate the birthday of the Church, the day when the Holy Spirit blew the doors off the room where Christ's followers were assembled.

This Sunday at Mass, thank God for the gift of the Spirit, through whom we can always have Jesus in our midst. Look around and see Jesus not only in the Eucharist but also in the *word* in the readings, in the priest celebrating the Mass and speaking His words, and in the community of people around you, the body of Christ.

"I am with you always," He says. Believe it!

Salvation Given

I am with you always, to the close of the age.

MATTHEW 28:20

Remember, when it comes to Church, you're *never* too bad to come in, and you're not too good to stay out.

Come, Holy Spirit.

Is the Catholic Mass in the Bible?
There's the Good News ... and no bad news.

The next sabbath almost the whole city gathered to hear the word of God.

ACTS 13:44

Situation Explained

Have you ever been told that the Catholic Mass is not biblical? I was talking to a really good friend the other day who told me, "The Catholic Mass is absolutely unbiblical, and it focuses only on the 'priest' and 'the bread wafers' and not on God's Word." Have you ever been faced with a situation like this one?

Solution Offered

Did you know that the entire Mass from start to finish is *completely* based on and founded in Scripture? Virtually every prayer and response we say during the celebration of Mass is based on the Word of God. Rather than beg you or anyone else to believe me, I'll give you just a few examples:

- In the name of the Father, and of the Son, and of the Holy Spirit (Mt 28:19).
- Amen (1 Chr 16:36).
- The grace of our Lord Jesus Christ, the love of God, and the fellowship of the Holy Spirit be with you (see 2 Cor 13:14).
- The Lord be with you (Ru 2:4).
- Glory to God in the highest, and peace to His people on earth (see Lk 2:14).
- Blessed be God forever (see Ps 68:36).
- May the Lord accept the sacrifice at your hands (see Ps 50:23).
- Lift up your hearts; we lift them up to the Lord (see Lam 3:41).
- Let us give thanks to the Lord our God (see Col 3:17).

- Hosanna in the highest; blessed is He who comes in the name of the Lord (see Mk 11:9-10).
- Let us proclaim the mystery of our faith (see 1 Tm 3:16).
- Christ has died, Christ is risen, Christ will come again (see 1 Cor 15:3-5; Rv 22:12).
- Lord, you are holy indeed, the fountain of all holiness (see 2 Mc 14:36).
- From age to age ... from east to west (see Ps 103:17; 113:3).
- Through Him, with Him, in Him (see Rom 11:36).
- This is the Lamb of God; happy are we who are called to His table (see Rv 19:9).

Hopefully you can now trust that there wasn't this bunch of priests sitting around a monastery a couple thousand years ago, making up random prayers like some wanna-be Hallmark convention. Let's give the Holy Spirit some credit, huh?

Our Church, the *universal* (Catholic) faith—founded by Christ, led by the Spirit, and entrusted to Peter—is *the oldest* Christian religion. Our Mass, celebrated in countless languages around the world, hundreds of thousands of times a day, with the same readings, is totally, absolutely, unequivocally, 100 percent founded in Scripture.

Take pride in the fact that you're part of a long and glorious tradition, and be proud to be Catholic! The apostles were.

Salvation Given

The next sabbath almost the whole city gathered to hear the word of God.

Acts 13:44

Go in peace to love and serve the Lord (Lk 7:50; 2 Chr 35:3).

Ever Misbehave in Church?
Dad doesn't look happy.

My son, do not regard lightly the discipline of the Lord nor lose courage ... for the Lord disciplines him whom he loves.

HEBREWS 12:5-6

Situation Explained

Ever get into trouble in church as a kid? I did—*a lot.*

Solution Offered

When I was still pretty little, there were several rules that my parents set for my brothers and sister and me before we entered Mass on Sunday.

1. Pay attention.
2. No talking, punching, pinching, shoving, slapping, or "wet willies."
3. No toys that made noise.
4. No standing on the kneelers.
5. No fighting over who got to put the money in the collection basket.
6. No trying to crush or break your brother's toes when putting the kneeler down (This rule had to be added following "the incident.")
7. No gum.
8. No crawling underneath the pew.
9. No trying to make your brother, the altar server, laugh.
10. And finally, certain brothers were *never,* under *any* circumstances, allowed to sit next to each other.

Now, these rules, for the most part, worked. They allowed everyone in our family and around us to actually hear what was being read, said, sung, and prayed at Mass. We knew that we had crossed a line either when my mother called us by our first *and* middle name or when my father stood up (and no one else in church did), took us by the arm, and walked us outside to have a ... well ... a "conversation."

Discipline. Through my father's disciplining us, we learned to discipline ourselves. That's love.

God loves us *so* much that He set up rules and guidelines to help us live every day, knowing that through discipline we would come to know, follow, and love Him more deeply. My father never enjoyed pulling us out of church, but he did know a couple of things:

1. What was happening in God's house was important for us (and for the people around us) to see and hear.
2. The same word in Latin that we get *discipline* from, we get *disciple* from.

I can't be a true disciple of Christ if I'm not *disciplined* in my prayer life, in reading my Bible, in attending Mass, in getting to Reconciliation, in sharing the gospel, and in serving others. Discipline yourself in your faith journey, and embrace the loving discipline and structure that God the Father offers us daily and that Christ Himself accepted.

Salvation Given

My son, do not regard lightly the discipline of the Lord nor lose courage ... for the Lord disciplines him whom he loves.

HEBREWS 12:5-6

Thanks for looking out for me, Dad (*Abba*).

Why Do We Genuflect?
Get on your knees.

A leper came to him beseeching him, and kneeling said to him, "If you will, you can make me clean." Moved with pity, he stretched out his hand and touched him, and said to him, "I will; be clean."

MARK 1:40-41

Situation Explained

Every Sunday, millions of people enter Catholic churches around the world. We bless ourselves with holy water, greet one another (hopefully), spot an empty seat, and, before we sit, we, hopefully, genuflect (kneel on one knee) to Jesus, present in the tabernacle. Why?

Solution Offered

The phrase "kneeling down" in some Bible translations is written "on bended knee," which is written *genu flexo* in Latin. Does that term look familiar? *Genu flexo* or "genuflect."

You see, the leper kneels before Christ as a sign of honor, worship, and respect, uttering his faith in Jesus' ability to heal him. This is a biblical example of why we are expected to genuflect when we pass by the tabernacle (if it's located in the church) and when we are before the Blessed Sacrament. We are just like the leper, in need of Jesus' healing. We bend on one knee to show Jesus, Who is *truly* present in the Eucharist, our honor for Him.

Unfortunately, nowadays, not many people genuflect when entering the pew before Mass, and few people show Christ the respect He deserves when passing by the tabernacle. A lot of people just don't know—a fact that those of us who *do* know need to get better at sharing with others.

I've often heard people say that "we don't need to genuflect" because Christ is present in the community assembled and in the Word. According to this line of reasoning, we would need to genuflect to everyone in church if we wanted to show Christ honor. While it is true that Christ is present within us, it is a mistake to consider that presence equal to Christ's *true* and *unique* presence in the Eucharist.

Some folks say that a bow is just as good as taking a knee. There are a lot of reasons why the Church says we should bend at the knee instead, but to put it simply, a bow doesn't "say" what genuflecting says.

Sometimes we also bow to people, but to get down on our knees—now, *that* is a gesture that is reserved for God. The psalmist says not just that we should "bow down" before God, but that we should "kneel before the Lord our Maker" (see Ps 95:6).

This might seem minor to some of us, others of us might "forget," and still others might not have learned the habit of genuflecting when passing before Jesus in the Eucharist. If you fit in any of these categories, don't be mad at yourself. But be aware now. Let those around you see the belief and the reverence you have for Jesus, *truly* present in the Eucharist.

Salvation Given

A leper came to him beseeching him, and kneeling said to him, "If you will, you can make me clean." Moved with pity, he stretched out his hand and touched him, and said to him, "I will; be clean."

MARK 1:40-41

A woman at my parish is 102 years old, and *she* still genuflects. That's not easy at her age. Now, that's a pretty cool example. Think about it.

Are Catholics Allowed to Sing at Mass?
"Getting back" at God with the voice He gave me.

David and all Israel danced before God with all their might, singing to the accompaniment of lyres, harps, tambourines, cymbals, trumpets.

1 CHRONICLES 13:8, JB

Situation Explained

What is your normal experience at Mass? Does Mass usually start at six o'clock *sharp* and end at seven o'clock *dull*? Have you ever wanted to scream at Mass because a lot of the people "just aren't into it"? What are you called to do at Mass?

Solution Offered

So today we have this verse from 1 Chronicles (which isn't exactly a book anybody reads every day), and we have an incredible example of a disciple of God.

Here's David—*King* David, the most powerful man in Israel at the time—*dancing* and *singing* with great enthusiasm. Let me write that again, because it's just that important. *King* David, leader of all Israel, was *so* overcome with enthusiasm and love for God that he sang and danced before God. Now, that's joy and that's passion.

Is that how you feel when you're before God during the celebration of the Holy Mass? When you look upon Christ in the Eucharist and encounter Christ in the readings, do you stop to think about how cool it is that you are experiencing God, the Creator of the universe—of the earth, the heavens, and you and me?

Notice two things here: First, David didn't care what people thought. He was celebrating God's existence and God's love for him.

Second, David was a leader in love with God who led others by his example. It says in the verse that all of Israel joined in the dancing.

We as Catholics have been fortunate to have a leader like this in Pope John Paul II. He is in love with God, and he leads us by an incredible example. One need only listen to his enthusiasm when he speaks, especially at the World Youth Days.

Start praying today, and pray every day this week, that this Sunday you will have a new passion for God. It may mean that you will need to sing louder, or sit away from distractions—maybe even in one of the first couple pews. Do whatever it takes to put yourself in a position to get more out of Mass this weekend and to lead others by your passionate participation. You don't have to be jumping up and down (that could be dangerous), but you are called to *full, conscious, active* participation.

Catholicism is *not* a spectator sport.

Salvation Given

David and all Israel danced before God with all their might, singing to the accompaniment of lyres, harps, tambourines, cymbals, trumpets.

1 CHRONICLES 13:8, JB

Why do we fight for front row seats at concerts but for seats in the back at church?

Lord, give me the desire to be a "front row" Catholic.

Ever Forget to Think Before You Speak?
What am I saying?

For all the promises of God find their Yes in him. That is why we utter the Amen through him, to the glory of God.

2 CORINTHIANS 1:20

Situation Explained

Do you ever speak without thinking? (Wait, think before you answer.) Do you ever say something before you really stop to think about what it means? (Are you two-for-two on this quiz so far?) Me, too.

Solution Offered

In the Gospel of Matthew, Jesus says the word *Amen* about thirty times.

In the course of a normal Sunday Mass, we say or sing the word *Amen* between ten and twenty times.

Amen is a derivative of the Hebrew word *aman,* which means "to confirm" or "to strengthen." When we say *Amen,* we are proclaiming something. We are professing our strongest belief, with all of our Christian soul. We are saying, "Yes, I *believe!*"

Not me. I can honestly say that most of the time when I say *Amen,* I'm not stopping to think about what I'm saying. I usually say it as more of a reaction than a response, as a way of kind of "ending" a prayer and moving on.

Well, that changes today.

When I finish making the sign of the cross, I'm gonna proclaim, "Amen!"—sort of like a spiritual "high five" to God, telling Him, "I'm right here with ya', Big Guy, and You can count on me, because *I do believe."*

When the entire church erupts into the Great Amen at Mass this weekend, I'm gonna sing it so loud that the person next to me will think I have a screw loose. And when I proceed forward to encounter and receive our Lord in His Most Holy Eucharist, and the Eucharistic minister says to me, "The Body of Christ," my *Amen* response will be strong and determined. My *Amen* will leave no doubt in anyone who hears me that I belong to Christ, that I am proud to be a Catholic, and that I believe in Him. I have met Him in His sacraments, in His *Word,* and in His children here on earth.

Who's with me?

Let's never again allow our *Amen* to be a reaction instead of a response.

Salvation Given

For all the promises of God find their Yes in him. That is why we utter the Amen through him, to the glory of God.

2 CORINTHIANS 1:20

Amen?

Are There Any Saints in Your Church?
For something that's stained, it sure is beautiful.

While you have the light, believe in the light, that you may become sons of light.

JOHN 12:36

Situation Explained

What is the purpose of the stained glass windows in church? Ever think about it?

In case you've never heard the following story, I wanted to share it with you.

Solution Offered

It was Sunday morning, and as always, a young family made their way into Mass. A beautiful little six-year-old girl, the youngest, sat amazed, gazing up at the ceilings, the candles, the statues, and the crucifix.

Then she noticed an incredible array of colored light beaming onto the floor in front of her. Her eyes immediately scaled the walls to find the source. She saw the brilliant, early morning sun shining through the stained glass window.

She asked her father, "Daddy, who are those people in the colored windows?"

"Those are the saints, sweetheart, people who lived for God and who loved Him very much."

The young girl nodded in approval. She kept her eyes glued to the stained glass for the remainder of the Mass.

A couple years later the same girl sat in her Catholic elementary school religion class. "Who are the saints?" the teacher asked the students at the beginning of the lesson. No one in class raised a hand, with the exception of the little girl. The teacher called on her, and she humbly rose to answer the question.

"So, who are the saints?" the teacher asked again.

"The saints are the ones the light shines through," the little girl innocently replied.

Remember, the saints were ordinary people who got tired, who got hungry, who even got annoyed. They got sick, they got headaches, they made mistakes, they sinned, and they went through temptations, too—just like you and me. They dealt with the same types of situations, people, and annoyances that you and I struggle with every day. The big difference is *how* they responded to God's call and *how* they chose to live in the midst of hardship.

You can be a saint. I could be a saint. We are all *called* to be saints. Don't ever think, "That could never be me." It can be you; "with God nothing will be impossible" (Lk 1:37).

Start today. Smile. Serve. Affirm. Let the joy of Christ radiate within you. Really try, in a new way, to *allow* the light of Christ, the awesomeness of God, to shine through you—to the wonder and amazement of all who see it.

That would be a beautiful gift, one that shouldn't be reserved just for church.

Salvation Given

While you have the light, believe in the light, that you may become sons of light.

JOHN 12:36

Make your life a "stained glass" work of art to a world in need of more beauty.

Do You Know Any Famous People?

Who sits next to you at Mass?

For where two or three are gathered in my name, there am I in the midst of them.

MATTHEW 18:20

Situation Explained

Do any "famous people" go to your church?

Solution Offered

I received a phone call last week from a friend of mine—we'll call him Tim—who works for a local TV news station. He wanted to do a story on all of the people "returning to God and filling churches since the tragedy on September 11, 2001."

"Great idea," I told him.

"Now, are you expecting *really* big crowds?" he asked. "Because we want to get good shots with the camera. Oh, and are there gonna be any famous people there?"

"Do you mean *besides* God?" I responded.

"C'mon, BG, you know what I mean," he replied.

"And you know what I mean, Tim," I followed.

You see, Tim and I were in the same youth group, and we used to talk about God all the time. But at some point (like so many others we care about) he just stopped coming to church. So when he called and asked to do the story, I had to just look up to the sky, smile, and laugh, because I felt like God was giving me another chance with Tim. (God is so cool that way.) I decided to take this opportunity to make him think about his question in a new way.

"Famous people? You want famous people?" I asked him.

"Yeah, the more the better," he replied.

"Well, I'd be happy to introduce you to the Blessed Virgin Mary, St. Francis, St. Thérèse, St. Maximilian Kolbe, St. Maria Goretti, St. Jerome, and St. Paul, for starters. They, along with the rest of the communion of saints, are at each and every Mass, and I usually ask them to sit next to me and pray with me. I'm sure they'd 'scoot down' the pew and make some room for you."

He laughed, and we talked a little bit. He was beginning to "get it." That Sunday he came and did the story, and we had a great conversation afterwards. In fact, he came to church again the following weekend.

While all stories don't end up like this, some *do* and other stories still might.

There are a lot of people, even Catholics who go to Mass religiously (pun intended), who aren't "into it" because they do not understand fully what's going on. You and I can change that, by striving to learn more about *why* we do what we do at Mass.

There's plenty of space at God's dining room table (altar). Now all people need is the invitation. Have you sent yours out? I've been a little lazy myself lately, but that's all gonna change.

Salvation Given

For where two or three are gathered in my name, there am I in the midst of them.

MATTHEW 18:20

Jesus—He's there every week. And that's why I am, too.

Godfather: The Role of a Lifetime
I wonder what God thought of the movie version.

We will not hide them from their children, but tell to the coming generation the glorious deeds of the Lord,... the wonders which he has wrought.

PSALM 78:4

Situation Explained

Who taught you how to pray? When did you learn?

Solution Offered

There are few things in this world that I take more pride in than being a godfather.

Nowadays, for many people, the role of godfather or god-mother is little more than a nice "honorary distinction" to place on a relative or loved one. That's a shame. It's a role and responsibility that I take very seriously, pray about often, and always try to answer with complete faithfulness and enthusiasm.

Why am I telling you all of this? Because although *my* role includes helping raise my godchildren in the faith, it is one godchild, my niece, who ends up teaching *me* a lot of the time. And she's only seven years old.

I was swimming with her over the weekend. She was telling me about school, sports, the boy at school who tried to kiss her. (As for that boy, well, he and I will be having a "little talk.") She also recited the Hail Mary for me and the Our Father, which she has almost perfect.

Well, she wasn't just "reciting" the prayers; she was saying them with joy. And she was watching my face the entire time, to see if her godfather (and uncle) was as proud of her as she was of herself.

I was very proud—not just proud of her but of her parents who are trying to share the faith with her. They are living out what today's verse is speaking about. It's not just in prayers, either. It is in her attitude, her manners, her awareness of what is right and wrong, polite and impolite. It doesn't mean that she doesn't "cross the line" but that she realizes that "the line" exists. That line is what separates the true Christian from someone who claims to be a Christian but refuses to live as one on a daily basis.

As I fell asleep that night, I said an Our Father and a Hail Mary as part of my prayers. I smiled the whole time. It seemed to "mean a little more."

Once again, it was the *child* who reminded this adult what it's all about. But then, Jesus always understood that (see Mk 10:13-16).

Salvation Given

We will not hide them from their children, but tell to the coming generation the glorious deeds of the Lord,... the wonders which he has wrought.

PSALM 78:4

To my niece, if you read this some day: Your godfather is a better Catholic Christian today because of *you*. Thank you for that gift.

Why Do I Need to Confess *That?*
It doesn't hurt anyone but me.

If any one has caused pain, he has caused it not to me, but in some measure ... to you all.

2 CORINTHIANS 2:5

Situation Explained

Who do my sins hurt? Who do your sins hurt? Only you? A popular misconception is that our sins hurt only us. It's common for me to hear someone say, "What's the big deal with (blank)? I'm only hurting myself." OK, I'll say this as lovingly as I can: *"That's a crock!"* Sin runs deeper than that.

Solution Offered

You know, at the beginning of Mass we say, as a community, "I confess to Almighty God, *and to you, my brothers and sisters,* that I have sinned through my own fault." Ever notice that we're admitting wrongdoing not only to God but *also* to the community of believers assembled with us?

Did you know that the sacrament of reconciliation didn't always take place in a safe little confessional box? Oh, no, get this: Everyone in the community would assemble at church, and at an appointed time at the beginning of Mass, one at a time, everyone would shout his or her sins *out loud,* in front of *everyone!* Stop and imagine that. Ya', it scares me, too.

What the people back then realized—that we don't realize

now or don't want to *admit* that we realize—is that sin hurts everyone. When I sin, it doesn't just hurt me; it hurts others, some whom I know about and some whom I don't.

Have you ever sat in the nonsmoking section near the smoking section? Sin can be like secondhand smoke. The sinner might not realize or admit that his or her "smoke" is having an effect on others. Those inhaling the smoke may or may not realize it, but the smoke *does* have an unhealthy effect. You see, once the smoke (sin) is out there, there's no way to control its effects or its harm to other people.

I have had a number of friends who think that if they "smoked out," or drank, or whatever, those decisions and their consequences stopped with them. That's not the case. We are all one body, those who realize it and those who don't. Our actions, good or bad, affect other people. All of our actions.

I took a hard look at my own life recently to see if any of my own "secondhand sin" might be making others' faith walks more difficult. The answer was yes, and I've had to make some tough changes. But by the grace of God and prayers from fellow Christians, like you, I continue to get better.

How about you? Any changes needed?

Know this, at the *very* least: I am praying for you. That I promise.

Salvation Given

If any one has caused pain, he has caused it not to me, but in some measure ... to you all.

2 Corinthians 2:5

Sin: torment-causing, soul-staining, hurtful, selfish habit.

Does Jesus Go to the Car Wash?
How dirty is your car?

A leper came to him beseeching him, and kneeling said to him, "If you will, you can make me clean." Moved with pity, he stretched out his hand and touched him, and said to him, "I will; be clean."

MARK 1:40-41

Situation Explained

You shower every day (hopefully), so *you're* probably clean, but is your car clean right now? How often do you wash the car or get it washed? Do you ever just wait to wash it, because it's just going to keep getting dirty, or because it's going to rain soon? I do.

Solution Offered

After I wash my car, I am *so* careful about where and how I drive. It's spotless and shiny, reflecting the sunlight (hopefully blinding the birds above who normally treat it as a target), and I want to keep it that way. I avoid construction zones. I avoid dirt roads. I watch out for mud. I go around corners more slowly so that rainwater doesn't splash up and dirty my car even the smallest amount.

Once I get some dirt on it though, all bets are off. I'm going through construction sites, I'm hittin' puddles, off-roading through mud bogs—I mean, who cares? I might even think about washing it and then say, "What's the point? It'll just get dirty again."

It's the same with my soul. Once I've reconciled with God

73

and have gone to confession, my soul is like my clean car: spotless, shiny, *reflecting* the true *Son* light. And I am so careful to keep it that way. I watch my language closely; I think before I speak; I avoid the "puddles" of sin at every turn.

Once I go through a puddle though, boy, it gets easier and easier to sin. "It's already dirty," I say to myself. Then when I think about going to confession (but don't really *want* to go), I say to myself, "Self, it's just gonna get dirty again," and I allow that to stop me from going.

Do you think that's what Jesus would say? It's not. Jesus wants our souls to be clean. He doesn't care if we "go to the car wash" of confession every day; He'd rather have us do that than drive around the car *He* created with mud all over it. Jesus wants all of us to be made clean. It is God's greatest desire to have us with Him, back home, in heaven.

At the same time, not everyone is getting into heaven. That's not a popular thing to say today, because a lot of people think "it's not nice" to say that some folks aren't getting into heaven. To them I say, "Sorry, folks, I'm just quoting Jesus" (see Mt 22:14; 25:33, 46).

Salvation Given

A leper came to him beseeching him, and kneeling said to him, "If you will, you can make me clean." Moved with pity, he stretched out his hand and touched him, and said to him, "I will; be clean."

MARK 1:40-41

Heaven's parking lot is full of shiny cars. And there's a space waiting for you.

Why Do We Go to a Priest for Confession?
Many faces, one Christ

Jesus said to them again, "Peace be with you. As the Father has sent me, even so I send you." And when he had said this, he breathed on them, and said to them, "Receive the Holy Spirit. If you forgive the sins of any, they are forgiven; if you retain the sins of any, they are retained."

JOHN 20:21-23

Situation Explained

Why do Catholics "have to go to a priest" to be forgiven? Have you ever been asked that? Why can't we just think about what we did wrong and say we're sorry in our minds, by ourselves?

Solution Offered

Think about confession for a second. Why would God want to humble us so badly by making us share our faults and sins with another person? Now read the above verse again.

Do you see how Jesus gives His apostles, the first members of Christ's sacramental priesthood, the power to forgive *or not* to forgive? This is vital for understanding reconciliation.

Say that you work at a gas station and a car pulls in for directions. Now, when the driver gets out, how do you know what directions to give? How do you know whether to tell him he's on the right road or the wrong road? Do you just *guess* where he wants to go based on looking at the guy, or do you *listen* to him first?

It's the same way with a priest during the sacrament of reconciliation. By necessity, a priest can know whether to forgive sins or retain them (as this verse from St. John affirms) only *once he has heard them.* Hearing the sins is essential.

But we still have the question of why go to a priest in the first place. Some of you might say that a priest can't forgive sins anyway; only God can do that.

Well, we need to understand the role of the priest in confession. We aren't confessing our sins to the priest, but to God. The priest is acting *"in persona Christi capitis,"* which is a big way of saying, "in the person of Christ." At that moment in confession, through the sacramental grace and power of the priest's ordination, the priest is standing in the physical place of Jesus. That's why the priest says, "I absolve you," and not, "Jesus absolves you." (It's the same during the consecration at Mass, when the priest says, "This is *my* body," not, "This is His body," or, "This is Jesus' body.")

Reconciliation is offered at about 90 percent of all Catholic churches on Saturday afternoon. Consider this a gentle reminder from your friend, BG.

I say it because I love you, but not at much as *He* does.

Salvation Given

Jesus said to them again, "Peace be with you. As the Father has sent me, even so I send you." And when he had said this, he breathed on them, and said to them, "Receive the Holy Spirit. If you forgive the sins of any, they are forgiven; if you retain the sins of any, they are retained."

JOHN 20:21-23

Forgiveness is always free, but that doesn't mean that confession is always easy.

E.W. Lutzer

Dealing With Life's Temptations and Trials

The high road to heaven has its potholes.

Does Life Seem Tough?
"Hey, God, ease up!"

God is faithful, and he will not let you be tempted beyond your strength, but with the temptation will also provide the way of escape, that you may be able to endure it.

1 CORINTHIANS 10:13

Situation Explained

Have you ever thought that God makes life too difficult? Think about it. Think about all those times you've been really tempted and have fallen because the temptation was *too* great. Think about all those days when nothing seemed to go right and you wondered, "God, why are you doing this to me?" When's the last time you had a day like that? Maybe even today ...

Solution Offered

First of all, as Christians we need to realize that there's a big difference between trials and temptations. Trials come from God, but temptations come from the devil and from within. How do we know?

Read the Scripture verse again. God *does not* want us to fail. He would never set us up to fail. That means that all those times we say, "It was too hard," after we've sinned, what happened wasn't God's fault but ours. This passage from Corinthians reminds us that God will never put us in a situation that we can't handle or survive, *as long as* (and here's the kicker) we have the courage and the humility to call on Him.

Obviously, if you're reading this book, you take an active role in your faith. Just as obviously, another weekend is coming up. A lot of Fridays and Saturdays offer us more difficult situations to respond to than the other days of the week. If you're confronted with a trial this weekend, have the courage to call on God, and He'll give you what you need to get through it. If you find yourself in a tempting situation, realize that it isn't God setting you up to fail. Live for Jesus in that situation, take pride in your faith and in calling yourself a Catholic Christian, kick the devil in the rear, and tell him that he can't win because you stand with Christ.

Salvation Given

God is faithful, and he will not let you be tempted beyond your strength, but with the temptation will also provide the way of escape, that you may be able to endure it.

1 Corinthians 10:13

Be proud of Jesus Christ. He's proud of you.

Does the Devil Really Exist?
"Hey, Satan! Beat it, loser."

So I find it to be a law that when I want to do right, evil lies close at hand.

ROMANS 7:21

Situation Explained

Do you believe in the devil? Are you scared of the devil? God isn't scared of the devil, and as His children, we have nothing to fear either.

The Bible tells us the final score of the game. Thanks to Jesus, we win, God wins, and the devil loses. That's why he's called "Lose-ifer."

Solution Offered

When I was in high school, I didn't believe in the devil. When I screwed up, I didn't want to blame anyone but myself. I used to think that I should be mature enough to take all the blame.

Let me tell ya', I don't think that way anymore. There are a couple of things I've learned about the devil that we all need to know and remember:

1. Satan does exist.
2. The greatest thing that the devil has ever accomplished is making us, you and me, believe that he doesn't exist. That way our defenses are down and we're easier targets.

Given these two facts, what is St. Paul telling the Romans? The devil keeps very busy, and the devil does not waste time. It's when you're getting closer to God that the devil works harder on you. That's why St. Paul says, "Evil lies close at hand."

If you're being tempted a lot in your life, that means that you make the devil nervous. It means that you're putting effort into your faith, and that's bad for the little lyin', back-stabbin', smack-talkin', guilt-givin', horn-headed, pitchfork-holdin' punk.

Be honest with yourself. What areas of your life are you weakest in? The areas that you are weakest in are the first areas that the devil's gonna take a shot at. Identify those areas, and pray about them. Turn them over to God, and let Jesus in.

Eternity is a long time. No, let me rephrase that: Eternity is a long, long, long, long, long, long time. The devil wants you to focus on "right now," not eternity. He'll even try to make you doubt heaven exists. Well, heaven does exist, and God wants you there!

The devil is gonna do everything to keep you out of heaven. Every time you're tempted, don't just look at the right decision as a way to make God happy. Look at it as a chance to show the devil that he doesn't have a shot at you. You're better than that, and you're stronger than that.

And you're *worth* more than you know. Your soul was purchased with Jesus' blood, and your love for God is your thank you.

God believes in you, and so do I.

Salvation Given

So I find it to be a law that when I want to do right, evil lies close at hand.

Romans 7:21

The devil is a loser.

Ever Feel Like You're Drowning?
Jesus, the Life Preserver

Peter got out of the boat and walked on the water and came to Jesus; but when he saw the wind, he was afraid, and beginning to sink he cried out, "Lord, save me." Jesus immediately reached out his hand and caught him, saying to him, "O man of little faith, why did you doubt?"

MATTHEW 14:29-31

Situation Explained

Ever feel like you're drowning? Ever feel like the waves of life are crashing in on you and you can't handle any more? Peter did.

Solution Offered

The comedian Steven Wright once said, "Tell a man there are four hundred billion stars in the sky and he'll believe you. Tell him a bench has wet paint and he has to touch it."

Why? Doubt and pride. Doubt is part of being human. Even though it's human, I'm always amazed to see how hard Christians are on themselves for having doubts about God from time to time. Doubt doesn't mean that we don't love God, and doubt doesn't have to make us weak.

Look again at this story from the Gospel of Matthew. Peter doubted. So why should we be surprised or get down on ourselves for doubting from time to time? I mean, *Peter* doubted (and denied) Jesus, and he went on to be the leader of the apostles, the first pope, and through the power of the Spirit convert thousands of people (Acts 2:41).

There was another great leader and hero in the Church

who was full of doubt and pride. St. Augustine was a pretty bad guy before he found God. This sinner was about as big as they come. After years of such living—and of his mother's prayers—Augustine changed and began living for God.

Augustine once said, "The reward of this faith is to *see* what we believe." What he meant was that after years of living for Christ, we will be rewarded in heaven, when we will get to see Him face to face.

The challenge is to not get down on ourselves when we doubt or lack faith. We're human, we're sinners, and it's normal. Even Peter doubted, and he was looking *right at* Him on the waves of the sea that night.

So what's the solution in times of doubt? Keep your eyes fixed on Jesus (and not on the waves). And *never* be afraid to cry out in prayer, "Lord, save me!" It's a sign of love, holiness, and humility.

Hey, it worked for Peter. Remember how the story ended: The very second he cried to the Lord, Jesus reached out and saved him. Pretty cool, huh?

Salvation Given

> Peter got out of the boat and walked on the water and came to Jesus; but when he saw the wind, he was afraid, and beginning to sink he cried out, "Lord, save me." Jesus immediately reached out his hand and caught him, saying to him, "O man of little faith, why did you doubt?"
>
> Matthew 14:29-31

A faith that hasn't been tested can't be trusted.

Adrian Rogers

What to Do With Stress
Just remember two things.

Be still, and know that I am God.

PSALM 46:10

Situation Explained

Do you have a lot of stress in your life? Do you ever get scared when you think about the future, or worried when you look at the present? Do you ever look up at the clouds, shake your head, and ask, "Why?"

Solution Offered

This is one of my favorite verses in all the Bible. I like to think of myself as a fairly laid-back person, yet so often I find myself allowing things of the world, situations that I have no control over, get me worried or stressed out. After a while, if I let them, these situations can really get me down and make me forget the Good News of the gospel.

Now, do I mean that we should skip up and down the streets, holding hands, carrying flowers, and singing "Kumbaya" or "On Eagles' Wings"? No, not at all (that is, unless you want everyone, myself included, to make fun of you).

It's OK to be concerned about situations in our lives. We're human. Whether you're struggling in school or in a relationship, having a hard time at work or at home, no matter how little or great the problem is, God is in control. He can handle it.

Whatever situation in your life has you at all worried, don't. Today God reminds us that sometimes we just need to pray and to *trust*. I mean what I say ... er ... write:

- *Worry* will drive you and me crazy. We're talkin' gray hair, losing hair, high blood pressure, premature wrinkles, ulcers ...
- *Concern* will drive us to our knees—to our knees in *prayer*.

Take the situation that makes you most concerned, and offer it up to God. "Be still and know" (and trust) that He *is* God.

Salvation Given

Be still, and know that I am God.

Psalm 46:10

Remember the *two* eternal truths:

1. There *is* a God.
2. You're *not* Him.

How Would Jesus Drive?
Is Christ really your copilot?

Jesus said to him, "No one who puts his hand to the plow and looks back is fit for the kingdom of God."

LUKE 9:62

Situation Explained

Ever taken a drive with Jesus? Ever seen His car? It is pretty enlightening, let me tell you.

Solution Offered

I was riding in Jesus' car the other day. He let me drive. Apparently He's used to riding copilot because His children always want to be in control.

Anyway, I wanted to switch lanes, and when I went to check the rearview mirror, I noticed that *there wasn't one.*

"Bro, where's the rearview mirror?" I asked the Messiah.

"You don't need one," Jesus responded.

"Why not?" I asked.

"Haven't you ever read what I said? Luke even wrote it down for you. Check it out; it's in chapter nine, verse sixty-two."

So, since it was good enough for the Creator of All, I figured I'd pass it on to you. Read it again.

"If you're *always* looking *back*, BG, you are gonna miss

what's in *front* of you, what I have prepared for you."

His words hit me hard, just as hard as this verse does. Many times I've lived in the past. I've even been consumed by it. I've focused on all of the things that I've done wrong—awful things, things that I had a hard time forgiving myself for, even though God had already forgiven me. I can carry more baggage than an airport skycap.

That's not how it has to be or is supposed to be, though, and that's why Jesus reminds us that we don't need to look back if He's with us, next to us, within us. If He's *that* close, we'll always be heading in the right direction, because *He* is the one navigating and steering, not us.

That doesn't mean that we just "blow off" areas or times when we've turned our back on Him or on others. It means that we seek forgiveness from God and from others and go on and learn from the mistakes so as not to repeat them. It means we make amends and move forward with God at our side.

Ask yourself, "Do my eyes spend more time in the rearview mirror than they do on the road?" Mine do. After that ride with Jesus, however, things are gonna change. He's the ultimate tour guide, and His car goes only in forward. With JC, there's no need for reverse.

Salvation Given

Jesus said to him, "No one who puts his hand to the plow and looks back is fit for the kingdom of God."

LUKE 9:62

God is like those objects in the side view mirror: *closer than He may appear.*

Can You See God at Work in Your Life?
Could you be more obvious, God?

*For this commandment which I command you this day is not too
hard, neither is it far off for you.*

DEUTERONOMY 30:11

Situation Explained

Where do you see God at work in your life? If you don't, you're
not looking hard enough. Take a serious look at your life
today, or this month, or this year. God is and *has been* at work,
in your life and in mine.

So where do you see God at work in your life?

Solution Offered

Have you ever heard that "the Lord works in mysterious ways"?
I have, and although sometimes God does work mysteriously,
I also believe that sometimes God is *obvious*.

No, I mean *really* obvious. No, we're talkin' "couldn't be
clearer if a lightning bolt hit me between the eyes" obvious or
"couldn't be more obvious if a voice spoke out of the clouds"
kind of obvious.

Speaking for myself, a lot of the time I make things more

difficult than they need to be. Sometimes, because I'm stubborn or because I want things *my way*, I ignore really obvious decisions in my life that need to be made, and I refuse to put God first.

I used to look at situations in my life that took my eyes off Jesus or my attention away from God, and I would try to justify them. I used to allow myself to be in "tempting" situations and think I would not be affected. Yeah, right!

Finally I admitted that God spoke to me very obviously—through the priest at my parish, for instance. He told me things I didn't want to hear. Through him, God told me things I *needed* to hear, for my own spiritual good. Then I started noticing God's voice in my youth minister, in my teachers, in my parents, in all kinds of people who loved me enough to speak the truth to me, the truth of Christ.

What situations and relationships in your life pull you away from God? Are you willing to make difficult decisions, even sever unhealthy relationships?

Listen to the words from Deuteronomy. God is not nearly as "far off" as He is obvious. Let's be honest with ourselves, step up, and follow *Him* all the way.

Salvation Given

For this commandment which I command you this day is not too hard, neither is it far off for you.

DEUTERONOMY 30:11

Remember, He gave us Ten *Commandments*, not suggestions. How's that for obvious?

In God We Trust?
Let go and let God.

Trust in the Lord with all your heart, and do not rely on your own insight.

PROVERBS 3:5

Situation Explained

Do you ever sit in Mass or go forward for Communion thinking, *"How* can this be? How could He *really* be in the Eucharist?" Have you been questioned by others about your faith and been unable to respond to some of their questions? Faith is a tricky thing.

Solution Offered

You know, Socrates once said, "True knowledge lies in knowing that we know nothing." Pretty profound for a guy in a dress and sandals, huh? He was right on, though, since for us to really encounter Christ in our lives, we have to be willing to admit that we don't know it all. We aren't God, and we all need help sometimes.

This verse today is simultaneously a commandment, a challenge, a wise suggestion, a proven truth, a difficult path, and a necessary exercise in humility.

Look around you. Look around your life. Look at all of the blessings that the Lord has bestowed upon you, things that you take for granted: your sight, your hearing, your ability to move, to walk, to run. Look around your home. Look at your family. Our lives and the people in them may not be perfect. But there are a lot of good things that most of us don't stop to give thanks for on a daily basis.

All of the questions you have, all of the struggles—get rid of them. Loneliness, anger, and hatred all weigh us down. God's message is very simple today; He's saying, *"Trust Me,"* and, *"Trust Me alone."*

We put our faith in all kinds of other things, especially ourselves. Now, it's not wrong to have faith in yourself, but there's a big difference between self-confidence and self-faith. The people with self-faith go to God only in times of trouble. That's not what God's calling us to do. He wants to be included in the good times, too, not just when things aren't going right.

Whatever your biggest struggle is in life right now, let it go. When you pray tonight, say to Jesus, "It's Yours; I can't handle it anymore." It may be tough to *really* let it go, but if you keep trying, you'll mature in your faith.

Remember, Christianity is not a spectator sport. Get involved; get in the game.

Salvation Given

Trust in the Lord with all your heart, and do not rely on your own insight.

Proverbs 3:5

Trust me. Uh, scratch that. *Trust Him.*

In Need of Patience?
The first thing I need, the last thing I want.

But many that are first will be last, and the last first.

MATTHEW 19:30

Situation Explained

When does your patience get tested the most? I know when mine does.

Solution Offered

Do you love waiting in line as much as I do?

I'm serious. There are few things we do during the course of the week that exercise our Christianity and make us use our Christian virtue of *patience* the way waiting in line does. We are a culture of people who don't like to wait. We like to have everything *now.*

Let me give you a few examples of what I mean. See how many you can relate to:

- Sitting in the left-hand turn lane, the light changes to a green arrow, but the driver in front sits in the car, not moving, not paying attention. Choice: Be patient or lay on the horn until the person goes deaf.
- Standing in the "express" lane at the grocery when the person in front of you wants to use coupons and pay with an out-of-state check. Choice: Be patient or roll your eyes so far back that you could go blind.
- Waiting to buy a bottle of water at a "7-11," the person in front of you has thirty-two separate items and "needs" to buy lottery tickets right then. Choice: Be patient or sigh so loudly that your exhales sound like a hurricane moving through the store.

- Waiting at the counter to order food at a restaurant, the counter employee talks to the person who calls in an order, who didn't take the time to drive there like I did. Choice: Be patient or make an unnecessary comment.

Well, you get the point.

I'm not saying it's always easy.

I'm not saying that sometimes it can't eat away at your last nerve.

I'm not even saying that sometimes situations don't necessitate action.

But that's what being a Christian in today's world is all about. It's not always easy, people *can* get on your last nerve, and *some* situations require action but not all.

Was Jesus speaking specifically about "lines" when He uttered this verse? No, not exactly. Would Jesus be a model of patience and restraint on a daily basis? You had better believe it.

If God has that kind of patience, couldn't you and I each be a little more patient in the heat of summer, when everyone's a little worn out? Or in the winter, when the sky is gray for days, the wind bites, and snow clogs the roads?

I'll try if you will. Start with today, and take it one day at a time.

Salvation Given

But many that are first will be last, and the last first.

MATTHEW 19:30

You need lessons? Call my mom. She's got more *patience* than a *hospital*.

Do You Ever Get Sick of Acting Christian?
Life's just not fair.

For God is not so unjust as to overlook your work and the love which you showed for his sake in serving the saints, as you still do.

HEBREWS 6:10

Situation Explained

Do you ever get sick of acting like a Christian? Do you ever wish that you could pretend that you "didn't know better" and do whatever you wanted? Do you ever wonder if God sees all that you do for Him or sacrifice for Him? Do you ever worry that He forgets or doesn't notice?

Solution Offered

In your opinion, is it more difficult to be a Catholic Christian when someone is persecuting you or when someone who isn't very Christian is "getting ahead" or "having an easier time" than you are?

Speaking personally, I can deal with people who make fun of me for going to church, or reading the Bible, or praying before a meal in a restaurant. I can even deal with people telling me that "Catholics aren't going to heaven" or that I "worship Mary and statues." That stuff doesn't bother me *nearly* as much as when the kid who cheats gets an A and I study and get a B; or when the kid who shoplifts has nicer clothes than I do; or when the guy next door cheats on his taxes and drives a nicer car than mine; or when I remain patient in traffic while the rude person next to me cuts in front.

Sometimes I want to scream, or I want to give the cheater kid a "swirlee," or I want to get the guy next to me by the neck and just ...

But then it hits me: Is that what Jesus is calling me to do?

It is really hard to be a Catholic Christian in today's society and live the way that we are called to live. No one is denying that.

I used to look up into the sky on bad days and say, "Hey, God, what are you thinkin'?" "Why me, God, and why today?" "I go to church, I try to follow You, and yet You're putting *this* in front of me to deal with? What did I do to You?"

Then it hits me even harder. God is *not* some evil, vindictive ruler trying to make my life miserable. Every trial that gets set before me is an invitation and an opportunity: an invitation to call on God and an opportunity to respond in faithfulness and *depend* on Him.

If you have those moments when you feel as though no one notices the sacrifices that you go through because of your faith, don't worry anymore. Make this verse your battle cry. Someone does notice, and that Someone is Jesus. God knows what we do and, even more, what we *don't do*. You and I will be rewarded when our time comes. The trick is to trust that God sees all and remembers all.

Salvation Given

For God is not so unjust as to overlook your work and the love which you showed for his sake in serving the saints, as you still do.

Hebrews 6:10

I'm countin' on You, God.

Ever Been Afraid of the Dark?
I need a night light.

But now the Lord my God has given me rest on every side; there is neither adversary nor misfortune.

1 KINGS 5:4

Situation Explained

Were you ever afraid of the dark as a kid?

Solution Offered

People suffer from different fears: fear of commitment, fear of loneliness, fear of poverty, fear of death. One fairly consistent fear for many, beginning in childhood and extending into adult life, is the "fear of the unknown."

What will happen with "this situation"?

What will happen with "this relationship"?

What will happen with "this job"?

What will happen with my family, my future, my ...?

When I was a child, provided for and protected by my parents, fear wasn't very common. At night, though, when I was in bed and my room was dark, with no one around, *that's* when I'd get scared. (Any of you who ever saw the movie *Poltergeist* can relate.)

Why? Because in that world of darkness existed the unknown. I couldn't see clearly, my feet weren't on the ground, and I was vulnerable. Somehow, though, after I prayed, I would fall asleep. It was as though my guardian angel was protecting me.

It's like that in life sometimes, too. The unknown can get a little scary, and being "vulnerable" to others or to God is not a popular concept.

Why, when the unknown confronts or scares us, do we not follow the lessons we learned as children? *Why* do we try, so often, to figure everything out or take control, rather than *trusting* in the fact that God is watching over us?

Jesus is the Light, the "night light" in the sometimes scary bedroom we call the world around us.

Any fears of the unknown in your life right now?

Well, handle it like a six-year-old: Say a prayer, roll over, and rest in the promise that God, the ultimate parent, is with His child. He is watching over you, protecting you, and guiding you safely through the darkness to the light of a new day.

Salvation Given

But now the Lord my God has given me rest on every side; there is neither adversary nor misfortune.

1 Kings 5:4

I pray the Lord *my* soul to keep. How 'bout you?

Ever Feel Like Everyone's Against You?
God's no quitter.

I have great confidence in you; I have great pride in you; I am filled with comfort. With all our affliction, I am overjoyed.

2 CORINTHIANS 7:4

Situation Explained

How often does someone compliment or affirm you? Do you have a lot of those days when you feel as though everyone's against you? Do you ever sit and wonder, "Are You there, God? Are You still with me?" He's always as close as an invitation, a prayer.

Solution Offered

The people in Corinth were in bad shape: pretty self-involved, pretty worldly, and not the most disciplined Christians. Yet, despite their faults and sinfulness, St. Paul (like Jesus) didn't give up on them. He encouraged them.

That's kind of the way it is with us, huh? You and I both know that we're sinners, that we're not perfect. Yet He *never* gives up on us. Why? No, seriously, do you ever think about the reason *why* He doesn't give up on us?

Like St. Paul, God has confidence and pride in us. He is filled with encouragement and overflowing with joy.

But, why? Well, that's where it gets tricky in this verse, so pay attention, folks.

The verse says that Paul is "overjoyed" over "our *affliction.*" Am I trying to tell you that God takes joy in your trials, in the things that cause you anger, that cause you worry, even that cause you to question Him?

No. Rather, what St. Paul's telling us is that *because* we have afflictions (trials) in our life, we know that God is at work in our lives. We should rejoice in our "afflictions" because they are a sign that we're maturing in our faith, that God knows we can handle them.

So when you face trials or difficulties, don't curse God for them. Thank God for them.

In 1 Corinthians we're told that God will never tempt us beyond what we can handle. We should have confidence that God won't abandon us when things get difficult; in fact, when things get difficult, God is that much closer. Remember the "Footprints" poem? It sums this idea up pretty clearly.

Just like St. Paul, I gotta say that I, the insignificant little Bible Geek®, have *great confidence* and *pride* in you. I am *thankful* that you've taken the time to read this and hopefully apply it to your life. If I'm this excited that you care about the Word of God (the most glorious of all words ever spoken in the history of creation), *just think* how joyful Jesus must be today.

If you have a lot of hurdles in your life today, say, "Thank you, God, for believing in me and for creating me smarter and stronger than I might want to believe."

Salvation Given

I have great confidence in you; I have great pride in you; I am filled with comfort. With all our affliction, I am overjoyed.

2 Corinthians 7:4

I've had a really tough week. God must *really* love me, huh?

He does love me. He loves you, too, and cares about you. And *so do I.*

Do Roller Coasters Make You Sick?
The minimum height requirement for fun is trust.

And which of you by being anxious can add a [moment] to his span of life? If then you are not able to do as small a thing as that, why are you anxious about the rest?

LUKE 12:25-26

Situation Explained

Do you like to be in control? Are you a control freak? Does "letting go" scare you?

Solution Offered

Ya' know, some of my *favorite* memories have occurred at an amusement park. As much as I love the park, though, as a kid I was always wishing that I were a little bit taller. I was usually just a hair too short to ride the really *big* roller coasters (even when I cheated and stood on my toes when the attendant wasn't looking). So I'd sit and watch as my older brothers got to ride the big rides, and I was stuck on the merry-go-round. Wow. Hold on tight. What a great time. (Hopefully you could hear my sarcasm in those last few words.)

Eventually I got to ride the roller coasters, however, and I fell in love with them. One of the things I noticed is the difference between the "ups" and the "downs." Everyone feels pretty much the same during the "ups." Everyone is excited or anxious, anticipating the fall. Well, the "down" is a different story. It's during the "downs" that people show their true colors. Some people close their eyes, some keep them open, some hold on tight, and some throw their arms up in the air. But it's always a rush.

On a roller coaster you can't "get off the ride." Growing from a child into a young adult into an older adult is pretty

101

similar. You just have to keep moving.

Life is like a roller coaster, not a merry-go-round, and the Christian life has more twists and turns than the regular ride. There are more challenges because being a *true* Christian means letting *God* control the ride—and not only the length and speed but also the height (the highs and lows). The fact is that in life there are a lot of things that we have no control over.

On the really difficult days, sometimes I wish I were "too short" again. It was a lot simpler as a child, wasn't it? No stress with school, or work, or money, or relationships. Let's be honest, though: The merry-go-round, while safer, gets boring.

What's occupying all of your thoughts and prayers today? What are you struggling with "in your heart"? Are you at a "high" or "low" point of the roller coaster ride of life? Remember, God is in control, and we never know when the ride is gonna end.

Today say "thank you" to God. Say a prayer and thank Him for counting you "tall enough" to ride the roller coaster. Even if you're scared (like I am sometimes), trust that you'll be OK. You're buckled up (He's the One holding you in the car), so raise your arms into the air and *enjoy the ride.*

Salvation Given

And which of you by being anxious can add a [moment] to his span of life? If then you are not able to do as small a thing as that, why are you anxious about the rest?

LUKE 12:25-26

You think life is exciting? Wait 'til you see *God's* Magic Kingdom someday.

That is a ride you don't want to miss.

Do You Ever Feel Like Giving Up?
We're not in Kansas anymore

He said to him, "You shall love the Lord your God with all your heart, and with all your soul, and with all your mind."

MATTHEW 22:37

Situation Explained

Do you ever give up? Maybe you should. (Now, don't freak; keep reading.)

Solution Offered

What's the toughest part about being a true Catholic Christian?

Getting *really* basic, it's a mind, heart, and courage thing.

So then, are you more like the scarecrow, the tin man, or the lion? Are you most in need of God's transformation of your mind, heart, or will?

For me it changes, almost daily. So why is that? How does that work?

Some days I *think* too much and don't act enough on faith. Other days I don't *feel* enough and wonder if God's "still around." And other days *fear* keeps me too quiet or too controlling, living for *my* plans or comfort rather than for those of God.

The solution? (If you say, "Click your ruby slippers together," we're gonna have issues.)

103

The real answer is prayer. Through prayer we learn to abandon ourselves in all ways: mind, body, and soul. It's like the song says:

Take my mind, and form it.

Take my heart, transform it.

Take my will, conform it to Yours, to Yours, Oh Lord.

Gotta go, I'm in need of a brain, heart, and courage transplant. I'm gonna swing by church.

Salvation Given

He said to him, "You shall love the Lord your God with all your heart, and with all your soul, and with all your mind."

MATTHEW 22:37

Make up your *mind* to speak from your *heart* with *courage.*

Now, I'm no wizard, but as a wise (yet cowardly) lion once reminded us:

What makes a king out of a slave? *Courage.*

What makes a flag on a mast wave? *Courage.*

What makes the elephant charge his tusk in the misty mist or the dusky dusk? *Courage.*

What makes the muskrat guard his musk? *Courage.*

What makes the sphinx the seventh wonder? *Courage.*

What makes the dawn come up like thunder? *Courage.*

What makes the hottentot so hot? What puts the "ape" in apricot? *Courage.*

What do *they* got that I ain't got? *Courage.*

OK, no more *Wizard of Oz* allusions. It *is* a good movie, though.

Walking the Walk

Catholic Christianity is not for wimps.

Do You Ever Cross Your Fingers?
Jesus "crossed" me, and I'm glad.

Therefore I intend always to remind you of these things, though you know them and are established in the truth that you have.

2 PETER 1:12

Situation Explained

What does the word *cross* mean to you?

I don't mean the Cross of Christ; I mean the word *cross*.

It's actually used pretty frequently in language today, but not always about Jesus. Whenever I hear the word, though, I think of Jesus. Stick with me here.

Solution Offered

The *Cross* is a sign of pain, of awareness, and of sacrifice.

The *Cross* is a sign of promise, of hope, and of safety.

The *Cross* is a sign of wisdom, of truth, and of victory.

And in the past two thousand years, nothing has changed. It's *still* a sign of all of those things—in many ways.

You see, if you

- *cross* your eyes, you'll be in *pain;*

- stop at the railroad *cross*ing, you show *awareness* of the dangers around you;
- *cross* something off your Christmas list, you're making a *sacrifice;*
- *cross* your heart, you're making a *promise;*
- *cross* your fingers, you're showing *hope;*
- *cross* in the *cross*walk, you're striving for *safety;*
- do the *cross*word, you grow in *wisdom;*
- *cross*-examine a witness, you get closer to discovering the *truth;*
- *cross* the finish line first, you get the *victory.*

The word *cross* has incredible meaning in our everyday lives.

So the question is, "Why didn't the chicken cross the road?" 'Cause it was a chicken.

Cross the road of indifference today. Blow off what the world says is comfortable.

Ya', it's tough following Christ, but the reward is *so* great. Don't lose sight of what God has prepared for *you* in heaven. It's incredible.

Take a step in faith. Trust in Him. He will not let you down.

Salvation Given

Therefore I intend always to remind you of these things, though you know them and are established in the truth that you have.

2 PETER 1:12

His was a blood-stained cross. *That* is how much He loves *us.* He wants your path and His path to *cross* daily.

What Does God Want?
God—the ultimate interior designer.

For we are his workmanship, created in Christ Jesus for good works, which God prepared beforehand, that we should walk in them.

EPHESIANS 2:10

Situation Explained

Did you know that God wants only *one* thing from you and me? It's not to be the smartest, or the strongest, or the prettiest, or the wisest. What does God want us to be more than anything? Give up? All right, since we're friends I'll tell you.

Solution Offered

What God wants from us, more than anything else in the world, is that we be holy.

Now, what does that word mean to you? To a lot of people, *holy* means quiet or solemn. Other people think *holy* means that you spend twenty-four/seven on your knees in prayer. That's not exactly what God is calling us to do. We know this from what St. Paul shares here with the folks in Ephesus.

Read the verse again. He calls us (you and me) God's "workmanship, *created* in Christ Jesus." That means that we were created, formed, and molded by God for a *purpose.*

Paul also says that the reason we were created was "for good works, which God prepared beforehand." That means that before you were even born, God had a plan for *you,* and that plan was for you to be holy and active in things that glorify Him and build His kingdom. Remember, it says "for good works."

An old priest friend of mine always used to say to me, "Fish swim and birds fly." Now, I know what you're thinking: "Wow, BG, very profound!" Bear with me.

You see, my friend meant that fish and birds give glory to God by doing what they were designed to do. In the same way, we humans give glory to God by doing what we are designed to do. We *do not* give glory to God by lying, stealing, getting drunk, or abusing our sexuality. We give glory to God by living lives worthy of the call that we've received. We give glory to God by living our lives according to a different standard, a standard of sacrifice and service, the standard of Jesus Christ.

The best thing about the call to holiness is that you never have to wonder what to do in a situation to please God; you just "do what Jesus would do." The person who came up with the "WWJD" bracelets owes St. Paul and the apostles. It was *their* idea.

Salvation Given

For we are his workmanship, created in Christ Jesus for good works, which God prepared beforehand, that we should walk in them.

EPHESIANS 2:10

The greatest contribution anyone can make is the example of a holy life.

Anonymous

Have You Ever Acted Foolishly?
I'm scared of clowns, but Christ isn't.

God chose what is foolish in the world to shame the wise, God chose what is weak in the world to shame the strong.

1 CORINTHIANS 1:27

Situation Explained
Have you ever been told to "grow up"? Do you ever just act a little foolishly?

Solution Offered
I was driving the other day with one of my favorite Christian bands blaring on my stereo.

It was a sunny afternoon, the top was off my jeep, and I was singing at the top of my lungs to the music (even when I was sitting at the stoplight). When it hit me that I was singing (very loudly) with the top off, I looked to the cars next to me. People were smiling, sort of laughing, and my first instinct was to be a little embarrassed. But then I got to thinking.

Who cares if I look like a dork? God sure doesn't. And I need to remember that.

For a long time I was really concerned with what people thought about me. Maybe you've even felt this way before. Maybe you still do sometimes.

As I grow in my faith, though, it becomes clearer and clearer to me that I'm not out to impress anyone, or "please" anyone, except God. Because if I'm *really* living for Him, everything else and every other relationship falls into place.

So that's why I'm the Bible Geek® and a "Jesus Freak" and any other name that gets thrown out there. And I'm proud to be, too. Let the world call me foolish or weak or any other demeaning adjective it can think of, because God can do amazing things with the weak and the outcast. Just read the Gospels.

What's "foolish" in the eyes of the world *isn't* foolish at all in God's eyes. He's more interested in the state of my heart and my soul than in whether or not I "fit in" with what is considered "cool" or "normal."

I wanna be a fool, all right, a fool for Christ.

I received some great advice once that I'd love to pass along:

Work like you don't need the money.

Love like you've never been hurt.

Dance like nobody's watching.

Words to live by, just like the Bible.

Salvation Given

God chose what is foolish in the world to shame the wise, God chose what is weak in the world to shame the strong.

1 CORINTHIANS 1:27

I'm with Christ. I'd be a *"fool"* not to be.

Seen Any of God Lately?
No late fees. Keep Him forever.

And now, Lord, ... help your servants to proclaim your message with all boldness.

ACTS 4:29, JB

Situation Explained

Seen any good movies lately? Experienced God lately?

Solution Offered

It never ceases to amaze me. I can be in a video rental store, in a grocery store, at work, even waitin' to tell the guy at the fast food place what condiments I want, and somehow I (or the person I'm with) starts talking about movies.

"Have you seen any good movies lately?" someone asks.

"I just saw the best (or worst) movie last night," someone offers.

Why is it that it's *so* common to talk about movies but not about God in everyday conversation? Why do we spend *so* much time recommending movies to watch but so little time recommending that our friends and family read the Bible or check out church?

Why is it that some days I spend *more* time wandering around the "new releases" aisle at my local video store than I do praying? Sad, but true.

It's not always comfortable to have conversations about God. It's not always comfortable to bring God into the work or school environment.

Why is that?

Maybe there's a comfort in "just recommending" a movie

113

and not God. *My* friends don't *have* to watch the movie. It's their choice.

It's the same way with God, though. Will people "check Him out" or "take Him home" based on *our* advice? Some will; some won't. All we can do is recommend *the* best title:

Jesus, *the* Lord, our Savior.

Maybe it's time I step back and rewind my life. It's time to take a look at me.

Am I ever ashamed to talk about God?

Do I ever *not* bring God up because I'm afraid it might make people uncomfortable?

What am I called to do? What am I called *today* to be?

Next time movie rentals or "new releases" come up in your conversation, think about *Him*. The person you're talking to might really benefit from a couple minutes of *the greatest* story ever told.

Salvation Given

And now, Lord, ... help your servants to proclaim your message with all boldness.

ACTS 4:29, JB

Coming *this* (and every) summer: *"God!"*
Two thumbs up—way, way up.

P.S.: Tozer once wrote, "What I believe about God is *the* most important thing about me."

Pretty impressive statement, *if* we have the guts to believe it, to live it.

Are You a Deep Person?
Jesus doesn't water ski.

The purpose in a man's mind is like deep water, but a man of understanding will draw it out.

PROVERBS 20:5

Situation Explained

In your opinion, are you a "deep" person? Do you think that your friends would consider you a person of great depth? How about your family? Why does it matter? Good questions.

Solution Offered

When I was a kid we used to go to the lake and the ocean a lot. We'd go boating, we'd water-ski, and sometimes we'd just anchor the boat and swim around or float atop the water for hours. I really enjoyed spending that time on the water.

As I grew older and (hopefully) a little more mature, however, my appreciation for the water *really* began to change. Going snorkeling and scuba diving the first time really opened my eyes. There was an entire world that existed beneath the surface I used to swim and ski across—a world of life, color, beauty, and depth.

Then it hit me. Most of my relationships at the time, especially my relationship with God, were "surface relationships" with no real *depth*. My relationship with my girlfriend, with many of my friends, with members of my family: all surface, lacking depth.

Maybe I was afraid to open myself up. Maybe I knew that if I did "go deeper" in my faith my life would get more difficult, or I couldn't "have fun" anymore.

God designed us and created us to experience a depth and a love that would make some people shout with joy but make most people wet their pants. Many people are afraid to "go deep." Letting down our guard, showing vulnerability, *forgiving* others, affirming one another, living for God and not ourselves: This is the "purpose in a man's mind" that the "understanding" child of God "draws out," as this verse points out.

God formed your heart, and the Holy Spirit that dwells there is not a "surface-y" type spirit. The Spirit is one of fire, passion, courage, wisdom, and love. Tap into It.

This weekend take off the skis, put on the flippers, and go deeper than normal. Tell someone how he or she has made a difference in your life. Speak to those around you as if it's the last time you'll see them. Take thirty seconds to *affirm* someone who needs it. That's the depth your heart was created for, relishes in, and is designed to share.

Salvation Given

The purpose in a man's mind is like deep water, but a man of understanding will draw it out.

Proverbs 20:5

On the surface I'm a geek. It's the *Bible* that provides the depth.

Are You a Dangerous Person?

I dare you to try this.

The apostles said to the Lord, "Increase our faith!"

LUKE 17:5

Situation Explained

What or whom do you pray for the most? If you look at the time you spend in prayer, how much is spent on you, on others, on stuff you want or need, and so on? Most people say that they pray but add that they "should pray more." That makes me wonder, "When we *do* pray, what are we praying for?"

Solution Offered

We need to be more like the apostles. I don't mean we should wear sandals everywhere (imagine those things in the snow), and I don't mean that we should spend more time fishing (that won't pay the bills). Today we just see the apostles being so simple and *so* straightforward with Jesus. Speaking for myself, I can learn a lot from them. I always seem to make my relationship with Jesus more complicated than it needs to be.

How about you? You feel like taking a risk today? You want a life of adventure? You want to live on the edge? You want danger?

If you don't, then *stop reading.*

Now for those of you who do: You can juggle knives, walk over hot coals, skydive without a parachute, leave Mass early (that's *very* dangerous), swim right after eating, run with scissors, play fetch with a tiger. Guys, you can even tell your girlfriend that you don't like her outfit. But if you *really, really* want to live dangerously, if you want to live on the edge, *pray*. Nothing in this world is as dangerous as prayer.

Why is prayer so dangerous? Simple, because our prayers can be answered. Lives can change, souls can be saved, and peace can be found—all through prayer. If we could pray for only one thing a day, today's request from the apostles would be a great prayer. "Increase our faith," they beg. Imagine if you and I had more faith in God—more faith in His plan (Rom 9), in His timetable (Eccl 3), in our future (Eph 2), in His *perfect* love (Jn 15).

You want to live dangerously today? Repeat after me: "Lord, I give you *permission* to work in my life and to use the talents you've given me to glorify You. Lord, I *dare You* to increase my faith and my desire to read Your *Word*. I dare You to turn my world upside down. I dare You to really teach me how to pray."

Salvation Given

The apostles said to the Lord, "Increase our faith!"

Luke 17:5

Catholicism is not a spectator sport. Get in the game today.

Are You Invincible Today?
All you need is a bed sheet.

[Look] to Jesus, the pioneer and perfecter of our faith who for the joy that was set before him endured the cross, despising the shame, and is seated at the right hand of the throne of God.

HEBREWS 12:2

Situation Explained

Have you ever wanted to be a superhero?

Solution Offered

During the summer I often think back to when I was a child, playing with friends until the very last glimmer of sunlight had disappeared from the evening sky and the bugs came out in full force. My favorite game (when I was about five or six) was when we'd each pick different superheroes to be, and we'd defend the neighborhood from the tyranny of the "bad guys" who lived in the dark (actually, vacant) house at the end of the street.

What amazes me now is how a simple bed sheet could "transform" me into an invincible superhero. That's all it took, a bed sheet tied around my neck. Once that sheet was tied, my arms went straight out in front of me, and I made a sort of "swooshing" sound and ran in circles—I mean, uh ... *"flew"* in circles—until I "landed" (making fists with my hands, resting them upon my waist, and then posing for a few seconds). Can anyone relate?

Well, a couple weeks back I was getting ready to go into a "not-so-nice" area of town to do a talk at a church. I hadn't been wearing my cross a lot lately (it's too hot in the summer-time), but that night I grabbed it and put it on. It caught my attention in the mirror for some reason, and I pulled it off and looked at it.

I realized, at that moment, that what I was feeling I hadn't felt since I was a kid playing Superman. I felt absolutely *invincible* again.

I had been to confession and Mass that day. I had spent some great time in prayer and learned some really cool new things in the Scriptures. At that point I *was* invincible, and that cross signified everything I wanted to stand for and everything I would give my life to defend.

For centuries after Jesus' death, the cross was seen as a symbol of defeat, of shame. It wasn't until the fourth century that the cross was seen widely as a true symbol of victory and Christian pride.

Since that night, every day when I put on my cross, I take a few seconds, look at it in the mirror, and thank God for the greatest Superhero ever, Jesus, *the* conqueror of evil and death. I also thank Him for the opportunity to follow in His steps, helping to "defend" my own little community from the "bad guys."

Superman got his power from the sun. What a coincidence. I get *my* power from the *Son*, too. And so do you.

Salvation Given

> *[Look] to Jesus, the pioneer and perfecter of our faith who for the joy that was set before him endured the cross, despising the shame, and is seated at the right hand of the throne of God.*
>
> HEBREWS 12:2

One difference between Christ and Superman: Jesus doesn't want His identity to remain a secret. Don't be afraid to tell everyone.

Ever Feel Like You're Being Watched?
Ten items or less ...

O my God, you search my heart, I know, and delight in honesty.
2 CHRONICLES 29:17, JB

Situation Explained

Do you ever feel like you're being watched? You are.

Solution Offered

A few years back I was in the checkout line at the grocery store. As I paid, and the last few groceries were packed into the bags, the young clerk handed me my change. I promptly thanked him, accepted the change, grabbed the receipt, and began to push my cart (with the annoying, wobbly wheel) out the door.

When I stopped to put the change in my pocket, I noticed that he had given me a dollar too much.

"What's the big deal?" I said to myself. "It's a dollar, right? It's *not* like it's gonna bankrupt the supermarket. *It will all even out.*"

For some reason, though, I turned, walked back to the checkout line, and interrupted the clerk, who was scanning the next customer's groceries.

"You accidentally gave me too much change," I told the young man, and I extended my hand to give him the money back.

"It wasn't an accident," he replied. "I recognized you from your church. A friend invited me to your Mass and LIFE TEEN program last week, and I heard you speak about honesty and integrity in your talk. So I gave you too much on purpose, and I watched to see what you'd do. I told myself that if you came back, I'd go back to that church, but if you didn't, then you were just like the other 'church people' who were full of it in the past."

I smiled, gave him the dollar, thanked him for holding me accountable, and told him I'd see him the next Sunday. He agreed, and sure enough, he was there—in the front row.

Now, I didn't tell this story to affirm myself, only to show how our actions and decisions, *even when we don't know it*, make a difference and affect other people.

Do your actions reflect God?

What separates the "good" person from the "great" person? In God's eyes it isn't the big things but the little ones. Let's never forget the challenge that Mother Teresa put forth to each of us: to "do little things with great love."

Salvation Given

O my God, you search my heart, I know, and delight in honesty.

2 Chronicles 29:17, JB

In God's grocery store, it doesn't matter what you look like on *paper*. He knows who is real and who is *plastic*.

Ever Spent Time in Prison?
God has my fingerprints; He put them there.

I therefore, a prisoner for the Lord, beg you to lead a life worthy of the calling to which you have been called.

EPHESIANS 4:1

Situation Explained

Have you ever spent time in prison? I have.

Are you a "convict?" I am—sort of.

Solution Offered

Convict is one of those words with a lot of meanings. We can say someone is a "convicted" person, and it doesn't mean the same as when we say someone "was convicted" (like, of a crime). My man Mr. Webster (the dictionary guy) defines *conviction* as "belief" and "the state of being convinced."

St. Paul was convinced. He was beaten, stoned, whipped, shipwrecked, and imprisoned. He wrote many of his letters while in jail. Now, take a second and think about that.

Paul is sitting in a jail cell, put there *because* he was proclaiming the Word of God, and what does he do? He spends his time behind bars *continuing* to proclaim the Word of God.

Paul was one "convict" who showed great "conviction." He was convinced. He believed.

When we follow the Lord, we might feel like we're "imprisoned" sometimes—imprisoned by a society that thinks Christianity is a sham, or by people who think Christians are weak, or by a culture that thinks Christianity is "outdated."

Paul's response? It's this verse: "Live in a manner worthy of the *call.*"

Paul didn't care how the world responded to his message.

People tried to shut him up; he spoke louder. They tried to lock him up; he wrote more.

It makes me ask myself, *how* convicted am I, really? Am I a prisoner of this world or a prisoner of the Lord? Do I "back off" or "ease up" when the situations around me get tougher? Or do I smile, try even harder, live even louder, laugh at trials, and tell the world to "gimme all you got"?

I want to be a convict for Christ. I want you to "book me, God."

And He has. There is a Book that convicts me. It's called the Bible.

Salvation Given

I therefore, a prisoner for the Lord, beg you to lead a life worthy of the calling to which you have been called.

Ephesians 4:1

Become a convict for Christ—not by breaking the law but by living *the* law that is Christ.

What Does God Want You To Be?
Does God have call waiting?

You did not choose me, but I chose you and appointed you that you should go and bear fruit and your fruit should abide.

JOHN 15:16

Situation Explained

God calls each one of us. Even though you or I might not *respond* to the call, the call is still there. Remember, when God calls, even if we don't answer, the call remains.

Never doubt that God is calling you. The real question is, *What's* He saying?

Solution Offered

God calls each and every one of us to walk in the light of Christ, live in the truth of the gospel, and be holy. Along the way He calls upon us to use the gifts He's bestowed on us for *His* glory, not for our own. He formed us and created us in His image.

As Jesus reminds us in today's verse, regardless of what we think, we didn't just choose Him but *He chose us.* He appoints us to "go and bear fruit" that will last.

No, He doesn't want us to go plant a garden, thank God. (I'm terrible at gardening, and I live in the desert.) He wants us to use the talents that we've been given to plant seeds of faith, to spread His Word, and to build His kingdom here on earth.

How do we do that? By being holy and humble followers of Jesus Christ, by being good daughters and sons, by being good husbands and wives. And for *some of you:* by answering God's call to religious life or to the priesthood.

All right, ya', I said it. Are you shocked? outraged? scared?

"Oh, BG, why would you *ever* suggest such a thing as the idea that *I* should be a priest or a nun?" Well, let me tell you why.

Not everybody is called to be a priest or nun or brother, but some are. Some of you reading this right now are being called! The priest shortage in the world today is not because God stopped calling people; it's because people have stopped responding, stopped *really* listening.

What's the answer? Simple. Not easy but *simple.* Pray.

Pray every day that God will make His plan for you even more obvious in your life.

Next, pray that you and I will have the courage to respond to God's call. If you've ever thought about it, don't blow it off. Pray about it, talk about it—and don't be scared.

Salvation Given

You did not choose me, but I chose you and appointed you that you should go and bear fruit and your fruit should abide.

JOHN 15:16

Gotta go. God's calling. He's got more than one line, so maybe you gotta go, too.

Where Does Your Time Go?
The blue ribbon for last place.

As each has received a gift, employ it for one another, as good stewards of God's varied grace.

1 Peter 4:10

Situation Explained

Do you spend more time serving others or being served? At home? At church? In the world around you?

Solution Offered

A few nights ago my best friend and I went to one of our downtown food shelters and helped feed the homeless. I'd love to say that this is something that we do regularly, but I can't. In fact, it had been a while, a long while, since I had been there.

We ended up serving almost a thousand plates of food that night, in little over an hour, to several very grateful, very hungry men, women, and children.

One woman, in particular, really caught my attention. Her name was Maria. She was a tiny little lady, probably in her early sixties. She looked so tired, her clothes worn out by the sun and the streets. This didn't affect her attitude or her personality, though.

"I'm Maria," she introduced herself.

I greeted her, introduced myself, and handed her some food.

"I haven't seen you before," she said in a thankful, appreciative, and loving tone.

Her observation hit me, though—it really hit me. She *hadn't* seen me before. There had been other opportunities to get down there and serve, but for whatever reason, I hadn't done it. "I've served enough today," I would think to myself sometimes, or, "I just don't have the energy." A lot of times it was true.

But right there it occurred to me that getting down to that kitchen and serving when I don't feel like it makes the sacrifice that much greater, and there is a grace I can receive with that.

I don't know how long I'll be around. Neither do you. Life is funny that way. Thank God that we believe in Christ and that we have His promise of everlasting life to fuel our fires of faithfulness. It doesn't have to be in a soup kitchen necessarily. Look around for opportunities in your own home, church, and community. Many of you serve already, and for that God is so proud and so thankful.

Just consider this a loving affirmation, reminder, and challenge from your brother in Christ, BG. I'll do it if you will.

"I haven't seen you before," she said.

"No, ... no, Maria, you haven't, ... but I guarantee you *will* see me again."

And she will, Lord, I promise.

Salvation Given

As each has received a gift, employ it for one another, as good
stewards of God's varied grace.

1 Peter 4:10

Thank you, Lord, for all those blessings I take for granted.

Do You Have Fun on the Playground?
Everybody needs somebody.

Iron sharpens iron, and one man sharpens another.

PROVERBS 27:17

Situation Explained

Have you ever ridden a "teeter-totter"?

Solution Offered

When my best friend, Ronnie, moved away when I was six, I had no one to ride the teeter-totter (seesaw) with. Yep, that was me: the pitiful kid sitting on one side, the other side up in the air. C'mon, picture it. (As sad as it is, it has to make you laugh.)

The teeter-totter depends on one thing: a partner.

And just as important as that partner is for a successful teeter-totter experience, so a partner is equally important for our daily faith walk.

I'm not saying that our faith depends on another person but that the small successes of our faith journey, on a *daily* basis, can at times be dependent on our ability and willingness to call on another, to share with another, to have someone hold us accountable.

Last night I got a phone call from a really good friend. He was faced with a tough situation, a temptation. In his time of trial he called me.

That's accountability: sharing your walk, admitting weakness, looking for help, and allowing someone to hold you to a higher standard, the standard that God has set for you.

I love this verse. It is one of my favorites in all of Scripture. It's more than a wise saying; it is a universal truth, a challenge, and a call to action. Just as you'd sharpen your sword by the iron of another, so you can sharpen your spirituality by another's.

The holier I am, the holier those around me can become by leaning on me when times are tough. And the reverse is true: I can become stronger and holier through the example of others when times in my life become more difficult.

Know and *trust* this: Life is not meant to be a solo act. The teeter-totter of life is gonna have its ups and downs. Find yourself a strong partner, and enjoy the ride.

Salvation Given

Iron sharpens iron, and one man sharpens another.

Proverbs 27:17

Dare to share your walk.

Who Are Your True Friends?
True or false: not an easy test.

Be on your guard toward your friends. A faithful friend is a sturdy shelter; he that has found one has found a treasure. There is nothing so precious as a faithful friend.

SIRACH 6:13-15

Situation Explained

Friendship is a tricky thing. There are, for most people, many different levels of friendship. Who considers you a friend? On a scale of one to ten (ten being the best), what kind of a friend are you? How do your friends rank?

Solution Offered

When I got involved in LIFE TEEN during high school, I basically had my "regular" friends and my "church" friends. It wasn't that the "church" friends were bad people, just that they weren't as popular or "cool" as some of my *other* friends, whom I hung out with more often.

After a while I began to realize that the people whom I respected most, trusted most, and could really talk to had one thing in common: They were the ones sitting next to me at Mass or on a retreat. My two worlds were colliding.

Ever felt that way? This verse is really simple yet *so* profound. "Be on guard with your friends," it says. Why? You and I both know why. We've all had friends who brought us down at times, even if we didn't want to admit it.

When you look back years from now, you might find (as I do) two kinds of friends that you remember: the kind who helped you grow and the kind who stunted your growth. I'm not saying that all your friends have to be "church" friends; just that when you have *God* in common, other stuff comes naturally, goes deeper. Read the verse again. Make sense?

Pick out one or two people who've been faithful friends to you, and email them, call them, send them a card—and thank them. Help someone grow today.

Salvation Given

Be on your guard toward your friends. A faithful friend is a sturdy shelter; he that has found one has found a treasure. There is nothing so precious as a faithful friend.

SIRACH 6:13-15

You've got a friend in Jesus (and in this Bible Geek®).

Do You Have a Busy Life?
Take your foot off the gas.

The apostles returned to Jesus, and told him all that they had done and taught. And he said to them, "Come away by yourselves to a lonely place, and rest a while." For many were coming and going, and they had no leisure opportunity even to eat. And they went away in the boat to a lonely place by themselves.

MARK 6:30-32

Situation Explained

Do you have a busy life? Do you have a full schedule? Do you sometimes feel that you just don't have enough hours in the day? Feeling a little stressed or overextended?

Solution Offered

In this verse Jesus didn't just encourage the apostles to pray but also to rest. They had been working hard, *so* hard that they hadn't even stopped to eat. Jesus is the ultimate manager of people. He warned the apostles that they needed to take some time off before they burned out.

How about you? Do you get *so* busy at work, or at school, or with sports or other activities that you push yourself *too* hard? Is *that* what Jesus is calling us to do? I hear constantly from people who are overworked or too busy, people who don't take enough time to rest or sleep. There's just "too much to do!"

Did the apostles have a lot of work left to do in their lives? Did they have plenty of people whose lives they needed or wanted to touch? You bet they did. Yet what did Jesus do? He *commanded them*, saying, "Come away ... and rest." He *ordered* them to rest. Jesus realized that if we don't take time out some-times and rejuvenate ourselves, we're no good for anyone.

On the seventh day even *God* rested. Who are we not to follow *that* example?

Jesus is giving you, as His follower, permission to slow down. Take it easy today, or this weekend, if you can. Take a retreat, or reschedule things and sleep in. Go rent one of your favorite movies, and take the phone off the hook. Read a book. Get out and exercise. Indulge in your favorite snack. Sit back and enjoy the world God created.

Relax, and don't worry, just for one day. You will be a better Catholic Christian for it.

Thank God the whole time you're doing it, and don't feel guilty. Rest up this weekend, because God has plans to use you next week. How do I know? Because God has plans to use you every week.

Don't get me wrong: Jesus worked hard. But in His wisdom He knew when to laugh, to sleep, and to rest.

Salvation Given

The apostles returned to Jesus, and told him all that they had done and taught. And he said to them, "Come away by your-selves to a lonely place, and rest a while." For many were coming and going, and they had no leisure opportunity even to eat. And they went away in the boat to a lonely place by themselves.

MARK 6:30-32

Our faithfulness isn't measured by a time card. Smell the roses. God created them.

What Do You Say When You Pray?
Words cannot express ...

The Spirit helps us in our weakness; for we do not know how to pray as we ought, but the Spirit himself intercedes for us with sighs too deep for words.

ROMANS 8:26

Situation Explained

Do you ever get frustrated when you try to pray because things just don't "come out of your mouth right"? When you sit at church or at LIFE TEEN or a prayer group and hear somebody else pray, do you ever say, "I wish I could pray like that," or, "I don't know how to say those things. I sound stupid when I pray"? Sometimes it can be intimidating to pray out loud, especially in front of a group of people, if you're not used to it.

Solution Offered

In this verse St. Paul is telling the Romans that it *doesn't matter* what words they use when they pray, because if they (like us) are doing it right (with our hearts, that is), then the Holy Spirit surrounds our prayer with its own language. Paul tells us that the Holy Spirit intercedes for us and speaks in sighs that are *too deep* for words.

God doesn't care what wording or phrasing you use when you're talking to Him. God knows our hearts. God knows you better than you know yourself.

Tonight when you pray, try something different. Don't be too concerned with the words—He knows all. Instead, why don't you do less talking and more listening?

Sometimes we just need to shut up when we pray. Spend some time in silence tonight with the Lord, and let Him really speak to you. Listen with your heart more than for a "voice." If you don't hear anything at first, it's OK; just stay silent. Let God do the talking, and let Him have the last word.

Salvation Given

The Spirit helps us in our weakness; for we do not know how to pray as we ought, but the Spirit himself intercedes for us with sighs too deep for words.

Romans 8:26

God gave us each *two* ears and *one* mouth, so we'd listen *twice as much* as we talk!

Finding God in the Everyday

He's everywhere … just take a look.

What Would a Commercial
for Jesus Look Like?
Jesus is not a channel surfer.

*He called them. Immediately they left the boat and their father,
and followed him.*

MATTHEW 4:21-22

Situation Explained

What would a television commercial for Jesus look like?

Solution Offered

The *denarius* was a Roman coin and the basic monetary unit
in first-century Palestine. So if someone made a commercial
two thousand years ago about following Jesus, it may have
looked like this:

Daily salary for a fisherman: *1 denarius*
Nets for fishing: *120 denarii*
Fishing boat with sail: *2000 denarii*
The chance to walk in the footsteps of Jesus Christ: *Priceless*
For a life without meaning, there is everything else....
But for life *everlasting*, there is *Master* Card.

139

Salvation Given

*He called them. Immediately they left the boat and their father,
and followed him.*

MATTHEW 4:21-22

Try the real *"Master* Card." You're preapproved, and the bene-
fits are out of this world.

Does Your Computer Ever "Freeze Up" on You?

The secret is to reboot.

The grace of the Lord Jesus Christ and the love of God and the fellowship of the Holy Spirit be with you all.

2 CORINTHIANS 13:14

Situation Explained

Does your computer ever freeze? Do you ever have to reboot?

Solution Offered

The other day I tried running too many applications on my computer, and it froze. What usually happens is that I get going too fast, repeatedly pressing buttons and trying to force my computer to perform too many functions at once. Then my computer tries to get me to slow down, quit a few functions, or restart.

Of course, what are we PC users supposed to do when the computer freezes? What three buttons do we simultaneously push?

That's right. Say it with me, CTRL + ALT + DEL.

It's the same in my faith life. OK, whether you're computer savvy or not, stick with me here.

In life when I get going too fast or try to control too much, I'm encouraged in little ways (by God) to slow down; "close" some programs that eat up too much space, energy, or memory (areas of my life not centered on Him); and start over or "reboot" (reconcile myself to Him).

Three buttons, *one* function, in order to change what's happening. And remember, the three buttons *must* be pressed simultaneously. No one button is more important than the other, since they're all a key to solving the problem.

This function can be compared to the functions of the Trinity (for our computer generation):

CTRL (control): By giving God all the *control*, I put His will before mine.

ALT (alternate): By allowing the Holy Spirit to lead me, I then live, think, and function in an *alternate* way.

DEL (delete): By my faith in Christ and through His grace, I can *delete* the effects of original sin and live in His image of loving service here on earth, hoping to share in His eternal banquet in heaven.

When we let go of all *control*, we *alter* how we live and think, and we *delete* possible death. We open the door to eternal life, where all other "functions" and "programs" stop running and *our only* function is to bask in the incredible love of God (never having to reboot again).

Here's one final thought for you Bible *and* computer Geeks, out there: The CTRL + ALT + DEL function works only on PCs and not on Macs. Maybe that's because it was the *Apple* that got us into this mess (in Eden).

Or maybe it's because when life closes doors, God opens *Windows*.

Salvation Given

The grace of the Lord Jesus Christ and the love of God and the fellowship of the Holy Spirit be with you all.

2 CORINTHIANS 13:14

Oh, and remember one more thing when working on your computer: *Jesus saves.*

How Often Do You Test the Batteries?
Rechargeable is the way to go.

*But as for me, I am filled with power, with the Spirit of the Lord,
and with justice and might.*

MICAH 3:8

Situation Explained

Do you go through a lot of batteries?

Solution Offered

When did I become so lazy?

Last week the batteries in my TV remote died. I don't mind saying it was devastating.

What was I supposed to do? Walk the eight feet to the television and turn the channels *by hand?* How absurd! I stubbornly moved the batteries around, slapped the remote control a couple times, pressed the buttons harder (like *that* was gonna help)—but nothing worked.

So I pulled one battery out. It had one of those little power measuring meters on it, so I touched the two dots and squeezed, hoping to see the reassuring message "Good" pop up in the window. Nothing—there was no energy left in that battery.

It got me thinking. If God put His hand around me and touched my head and heart, what word would come up? Would it read "Good"? My spiritual battery gets low on power, too, and sometimes may even seem dead. Of course, no matter how low it is, because of my baptism it can *never* die. It just needs to be recharged every so often.

The more I allow God into my life, the stronger my battery becomes, going from "good" to "very good" to "great" to "unstoppable." The catch is, I have to seek out the outlet (God) and "plug in" (*let* God form me).

If you're at one of those "low points" right now where you're not really excited about the faith or are having a hard time, then it's time to plug in and recharge the batteries.

If you're running strong right now, like some "energizer bunny of faith," then look around, find someone who needs a jump start, and help them to tap in.

When the batteries in my remote died I felt helpless, and I couldn't function. But when my spiritual battery is low, I realize how helpless I truly am. Coincidence?

Salvation Given

But as for me, I am filled with power, with the Spirit of the Lord, and with justice and might.

MICAH 3:8

Nothing outlasts God, He just keeps *going, and going, and going, and going ...*

Are There Telephone Poles in Your Neighborhood?
God's on the line.

He himself bore our sins in his body on the tree, that we might die to sin and live to righteousness. By his wounds you have been healed.

1 PETER 2:24

Situation Explained

Is there a telephone pole in front of your house or on your street? They're really not very common anymore, but telephone poles used to be in every neighborhood and on every block. Do you ever stop to think about how the phone works?

Solution Offered

Last weekend I was driving back home from out of state, and I found myself on a road in the middle of nowhere. Then I noticed something. Now, here we were out in the desert, with nothing around us at all, and the only sign of civilization besides the road were all of these telephone poles.

You see, nowadays, with cell phones and underground fiber optic cables, telephone poles aren't very common. When I was a kid, it seemed like there were telephone poles every ten feet, in every neighborhood. They'd always be covered with "Lost Dog" or "Garage Sale" signs. They would get in the way of our skateboarding and bike riding (that's why I didn't like telephone poles).

Have you ever really *looked* at a telephone pole? It kind of looks like a cross, if you think about it.

For a telephone pole to be effective, though, it has to be connected to other poles, right? I mean, a telephone pole, sitting alone by itself in a field, with no wires connected to it,

145

wouldn't exactly be useful, would it? It has to be tied into something.

That's the beauty of it, and of the cross, and of the entire gospel message.

You see, the gospel isn't meant for one or two of us but for everyone. Jesus came not to save a few but to save all. We are *all* tied into one another. We are God's family, brothers and sisters. Some we get along with, and some we don't (just like a regular family, huh?). We've all got our own cross to bear in this world, but what ties us together and ties us into God is the cross of Christ.

Think of the Holy Spirit as the power in the telephone lines, linking us to one another, getting our "messages" across to each other and God. What you do affects me, and what I do affects you. We are *all* parts of *one* body. We are tied together, brought together, bound together, by that pole, that cross.

And just as technology has made telephone poles not really necessary anymore, the world also tries to make God not necessary anymore. We are told to believe that Jesus wasn't really God or that the Resurrection was a myth. They can go on thinking that if they want to, but me—my eyes are wide open, and they see a cross.

Salvation Given

He himself bore our sins in his body on the tree, that we might die to sin and live to righteousness. By his wounds you have been healed.

1 PETER 2:24

Maybe that's why they call miscommunication "getting your signals 'crossed.'"

Ever Lose the Signal on Your Cell Phone?
God: wired into the wireless.

*Bring forth the people who are blind, yet have eyes, who are deaf,
yet have ears!*
ISAIAH 43:8

Situation Explained
Do you ever lose the signal on your cell phone while you're
talking? It's pretty annoying, huh?

Solution Offered
Some people call them "dead zones." They are the areas where
you lose your cell phone signal in the middle of a conversation. Talk about *frustrating*.

When it happens, I usually end up spending the next five
or so minutes moving my head and phone (an inch at a time)
in weird angles to try to regain the signal. It's usually a case of
the other person still being able to hear me, even though I
can't hear him or her. The conversation is basically "Hello....
Can you hear me?" and "Are you there?"

What's even worse is when I know that I'm about to drive
through a dead zone, and rather than pull my car over, I just
drive through it anyway and stubbornly attempt to keep talking (frustrating myself *and* the person I'm speaking with).

I have these "dead zones" in my spiritual life, too.

147

I can be doing great in my prayer life and in my faith journey, but then I actively do or say things that weaken my relationship with God. Deciding to "go through" a dead zone disrupts my communication with our Lord and the overall strength of my (spiritual) signal. I know He can still hear me, but I can no longer hear Him, deafened as I am by *my* wants and needs.

I look at the little bar indicators on my cell phone that tell how strong my signal is and think about how I kind of have one of those indicators imprinted on my soul, too.

I *know* when I'm choosing to enter a dead zone; I *know* when I can't hear His voice as clearly as I did before. The question is, What do I do about it? And when?

The bad news is that in my pride, I usually wait a lot longer than I should to do anything (dumb move).

The beauty of it is that God never gives up or hangs up. He waits, with patience, until I can move out of that dead zone and get to a better "location" in my life.

So next time you're on a cell phone with someone and one of you hits a "dead zone," stop, take a second, and say a prayer of thanks to God for never "hanging up" on us.

Salvation Given

Bring forth the people who are blind, yet have eyes, who are deaf, yet have ears!

ISAIAH 43:8

Speaking for God, like any parent, I think He's just really glad when we take the time to call.

Ever Try Being Quiet?
Like when you're looking for the cordless phone?

For thus said the Lord God, the Holy One of Israel, "In return-
ing and rest you shall be saved; in quietness and in trust shall
be your strength."

ISAIAH 30:15

Situation Explained

My world is really loud. How's yours?

Solution Offered

I lost a cordless phone in my house recently. That drives me
crazy. I ripped apart the main room looking for it, in all the
sofa cushions, underneath pillows. I looked for probably twenty
minutes, and several times I looked in the same place (I don't
know why I do that). I couldn't find it anywhere.

Finally it hit me to press that pager button on the phone's
base. I turned off the TV and the stereo, pressed the button,
and sure enough, I found the cordless phone "calling out to
me" from a place I hadn't looked.

It suddenly hit me that it's like that with God and me some-times, too. Some days I might look and look and look for God around me and, amid all of the noise in my life, not be able to find Him or hear Him. When I eliminate the noise, however, and "page" Him, I can hear Him calling to me out of the silence I've made around me. Make sense?

I'm one of those people who *always* need to have some kind of "background noise," whether it's a radio, or a television, or whatever. As long as there's some kind of other sound in a room, I'm happy. Now, that's *not* a bad thing. What *is* a bad thing is if I forget to take time (I should say, *make* time) for silence.

One of the most difficult things to do in this world is to spend time in silence. At the same time, it's one of *the best* ways to pray, sitting silently and just listening to God (rather than doing all of the talking—like I usually do).

Today make an effort, even if it's just for fifteen minutes, to be silent. Whether it's turning off the car radio or locking yourself in the bedroom, be silent for a little while. You might be surprised by what you hear.

Tune out the world, and *tune in* to God.

Salvation Given

> *For thus said the Lord God, the Holy One of Israel, "In return-ing and rest you shall be saved; in quietness and in trust shall be your strength."*
>
> Isaiah 30:15

Making time is like pressing that pager button: Just do it, and listen.

Would Jesus Chew Gum?
Blowing bubbles with the Creator

*[So] that through these you may escape from the corruption that
is in the world because of evil passion ... make every effort to supplement your faith with virtue, and virtue with knowledge, and
knowledge with self-control, and self-control with steadfastness.*

2 PETER 1:4-6

Situation Explained

Ever feel like your faith life is boring or has "lost its flavor"?
Ever wonder why?

Solution Offered

I love gum. I mean it, I really do. As a kid, I always had gum in
my mouth (and sometimes in my hair, but that's another story).

If someone asked you to describe what gum is like, what
would you say? How would you describe it? It's hard to find the
words, huh?

You'd probably say that "it's something with flavor that you
chew on." They might ask back, "Why do you chew it?" "Well,
the whole point of gum is to chew it." "OK, but *why?*" "Well,
that's the whole point of gum ... to be chewed."

Gum is kind of like faith.

When gum (faith) loses its flavor (excitement), we just throw
it out, because it's stale (boring), or we're tired of chewing
(putting in effort). The difference is that faith is like a gum
which the more we chew (put in effort), the more flavor
(strength) we experience—and we'll never throw it out. It just
takes *constant* effort.

Maybe you can't explain what your faith is like, only that you
know it's there and that it's *always* good to have a little with you

for when you really need it—just like gum.

Now, read today's verse again. What is St. Peter telling us to do?

1. Look around and *see the evil* desires in people and in the world that take our attention away from God.
2. Put *effort* into our faith.
3. *Supplement* (grow and mature) in our faith.

This doesn't apply just to teens or young adults; this is a call to everyone, regardless of age, experience, or openness. We're all on a journey of faith: Some are walking, some running, some standing still, but we're all on a path.

So *how* do we survive the evils of the world? Tell 'em again, St. Peter: effort.

That's right, effort. We need to mature in our faith by growing in virtue (leading a moral life), in knowledge (reading and studying the Scriptures), in self-control (controlling our speech, emotions, and, yes, sexuality), and in steadfastness (*never* quitting or giving up on God, no matter how "hard" it gets). That's how we grow.

Salvation Given

[So] that through these you may escape from the corruption that is in the world because of evil passion ... make every effort to supplement your faith with virtue, and virtue with knowledge, and knowledge with self-control, and self-control with steadfastness.

2 Peter 1:4-6

If your faith has lost its flavor, put in a new piece (reconciliation) and start chewing.

Ever Try to Feel Your Way Around in the Dark?
Sleepwalking the walk.

Your word is a lamp to my feet, a light on my path.

PSALM 119:105, JB

Situation Explained

Have you ever had to find your way around in the dark?
It can be tough, especially if you aren't exactly sure where you are going.

Solution Offered

So I woke up in the middle of the night this week, half-asleep and thirsty, and went to the kitchen to get some water. I wanted to go right back to sleep, so I was keeping my eyes closed as much as I could (ever do that?) and was sort of "feeling" my way to the kitchen. As I walked, I stubbed my toe on the wall. *Ouch!* (And that *is* what I said.)

It hurt really bad, but I didn't know how badly I had wounded it until I opened the refrigerator door. The light spilled out and exposed a very, very sore foot, swelling up and turning a lovely "bruise" shade of purple.

When I saw how bad the injury was, I quickly grabbed some

ice and hobbled over to the couch. There I sat, awake and in pain and annoyed that I had left my comfortable, warm, and safe bed to venture into the darkness, *too stubborn* to turn on a light. Good call, BG.

After hobbling into church for Mass the next day, I had to kind of laugh when we sang, "Thy word is a lamp unto my feet." Too bad I hadn't been carrying a Bible into the kitchen, huh?

It is an interesting comparison, though. The Word of God *is* a light in the darkness—the darkness of a world that can be pretty selfish and pretty sick at times.

As disciples of Christ we are called to go out into the world and preach the Good News of Christ through *not only* words but also actions. The world can be a dark place, which is why the Word of Christ is *so* important. When we hold the Word deep within our hearts and apply the truth of the Bible to our everyday lives, we not only *have* our light in the darkness, *we are* a light in the darkness. The better we learn and hold fast to Scripture, the less we will "stub our toes" on stupid sins. We will see clearly enough to avoid the walls and to know when to "turn corners."

Spend a few minutes in the Bible this weekend, and see what God is telling *you*. It's dangerous in the dark, but we have nothing to fear when we stand in the light, His light.

Salvation Given

Your word is a lamp to my feet, a light on my path.

PSALM 119:105, JB

In my house the flashlight is just a place to keep dead batteries.

I Didn't Know That Was in the Bible
Don't tell me that Catholics don't know the Bible

For ever, O Lord, [your] word is firmly fixed in the heavens.

PSALM 119:89

Situation Explained

A lot of people think that the Bible is an out-of-date book that has no application in the "real world." But I'll bet you and your parents have quoted Scripture at times and not even known it. Let me show you what I mean.

Solution Offered

There are a lot of common phrases we use today that have their roots in God's Book, the Bible. How many of these have you heard?

- The blind leading the blind (see Mt 15:14)
- Turn the other cheek (see Mt 5:39)
- By the skin of your teeth (see Jb 19:20)
- Holier than thou (see Is 65:5)
- A leopard can't change his spots (see Jer 13:23)
- The powers that be (see Rom 13:1, old King James Version)
- Keep on the straight and narrow (see Mt 7:14)
- Am I my brother's keeper? (see Gn 4:9)
- Keep the faith (see 2 Tm 4:7)
- The Good Samaritan (see Lk 10:30-37)
- Eat, drink, and be merry (see Eccl 8:15)
- Armageddon (see Rv 16:16)
- A wolf in sheep's clothing (see Mt 7:15)
- The writing on the wall (see Dn 5)

155

- The apple of one's eye (see Dt 32:10)
- A drop in the bucket (see Is 40:15)
- An eye for an eye (see Ex 21:22-24)
- Nothing new under the sun (see Eccl 1:9)
- A scapegoat (see Lv 16:8-10)
- Woe is me! (see Is 6:5)

Even a lot of non-Catholic Christians do not read their Bible every day. But the Bible is the best-selling book in history, published in more languages than any other, surviving countless people and wars that have tried to destroy it.

Unfortunately, many times people are right when they accuse Catholics of not knowing their Bibles. The good news, however, is that it *doesn't have to* be that way.

Reading this book of Scripture meditations is a fine first step, but you can't stop here. Crack open *the* Book. Then go on to the *Catechism of the Catholic Church* and other books that help you understand the Bible. Ask priests for guidance; ask youth ministers and *anyone* in your church who may know a lot about Scripture.

I never want to be considered a lazy Catholic, and I don't think that you do either. I pledge to all of you, especially to you teens, to open my Bible every day and read the Word of God, even if it's only for a couple minutes.

Who's with me?

Salvation Given

For ever, O Lord, [your] word is firmly fixed in the heavens.

PSALM 119:89

Here I am, God. I *dare* You to set me on fire for Your Word.

How Loud Is Your Radio?
God offers direction; I need to listen.

Listen to me; be silent, and I will teach you wisdom.

JOB 33:33

Situation Explained

Have you ever gotten lost when driving the car? Have you ever been given poor directions or gotten "turned around" when trying to find someplace for the first time? Me, too.

Solution Offered

It never fails. Now, I consider myself pretty good with directions, and I don't get lost very often. But whenever I'm in a hurry when writing down directions, I end up driving in circles.

And you know what I do when I'm driving and lost? I turn the radio down.

That's right. When I'm lost, I always seem to turn down the radio. Why do I do that? *How* and *why* is the radio connected to my ability to navigate? I don't know, but I always do it. It's as if I can concentrate better without the additional noise.

Look at this verse; this is God speaking to you, just as directly as He did to Job so many years ago. We *all* get "turned around" sometimes. We get going in one direction (which is probably the wrong direction), but the secret to getting where we *need* to be is "turning down the radio," silencing all of the noise of the world around us and just being silent.

If you're like me, you have a very busy life, filled with people who want or need your time and attention. It can all get pretty noisy, huh? Also, if you're like me, you probably don't take as much silent time as you could—time with no phone, television, or music around you.

Do yourself a favor this week. Turn off your radio when you're in the car, and just allow God to speak to you in the silence. When you're at home tonight, go to bed earlier than normal, before you're falling asleep. And instead of talking to God, listen to Him.

And sometime this week, don't tell anybody, but get to a church on your own when it's empty. Take fifteen or twenty minutes when no one's around. Sit in silence in the house of God. Let Him do the talking.

Whether or not you're "lost" right now, it never hurts to turn that radio down.

Salvation Given

Listen to me; be silent, and I will teach you wisdom.

JOB 33:33

God can be so loud in the silence. Try Him.

Speed Bumps Are So Annoying
My Life: God's parking lot.

I will instruct you and teach you the way you should go; I will counsel you with my eye upon you.

PSALM 32:8

Situation Explained

Ever feel like God is slowing you down? Do you ever get impatient with God and His plan for you? Ever tell God that if He'd just tell you what to do you'd do it?

Solution Offered

I was stuck in traffic the other morning and really annoyed. I was annoyed because I was in a hurry and had a lot of work to do, God's work.

I couldn't be slowed down for anything. I mean, "For the love of ... well, *Him!*" This was *His work!*

When I *finally* got out of traffic and made it into the parking lot, I got *really* frustrated. *Speed bumps.*

I hate speed bumps. I mean, I *hate* them. They're so annoying, and they slow me down when I have things to do.

I exhaled and began to get angry. Then I saw a dog run across my path. At that moment I was thankful for the speed bump. Had it not been there, I may have hit that dog.

Just then I had a realization. There are a lot of speed bumps in my spiritual life—*a lot* of little obstacles, little trials God sets before me to slow me down and force me to look around.

I don't know about you, but when I get going on something, I can get *so* focused on it that I don't fully realize what's happening around me. Sometimes I'm so focused on *my* life that I forget others and their lives—even my brothers and sisters in Christ, even my family. God knows I need to slow down.

Sometimes when things don't "go our way," it may just be one of God's spiritual speed bumps: a way of getting our attention, slowing us down, and helping us to refocus on the bigger picture of life.

The next time you go over a speed bump in a parking lot, *thank God* for every trial that He places in your life. Because each trial is an opportunity to grow closer to Him in trust, in prayer, and in love.

Salvation Given

> *I will instruct you and teach you the way you should go; I will counsel you with my eye upon you.*
>
> PSALM 32:8

Life is like a parking lot. Watch for the speed bumps; *they're there for a reason.*

Looking for God? He's at the Airport
Christianity: United and Trans-World

But from there you will seek the Lord your God, and you will find him, if you search after him with all your heart and with all your soul.

DEUTERONOMY 4:29

Situation Explained

Where is God?

Solution Offered

As I sit in an airport terminal with bloodshot eyes, waiting to board a plane, I begin to notice my surroundings. The morning sky is dark, and most of the city has not woken up yet (including myself). I decide that my morning challenge is to see where I can find God in the world immediately around me.

- I'm sitting at the gate. Hey, wait a minute. Jesus called Himself "the Gate" (see Jn 10:9).
- I had to plug in my laptop to get power—kind of like the power we receive as Christians when we "plug into" the Holy Spirit (see Rom 15:13).
- There's a cranky guy (who probably hasn't had his coffee yet) yelling at the gate agent. "Blessed are you (gate agent lady) when you're persecuted for righteousness' sake" (Mt 5:10).
- There's a little boy (who has apparently eaten a *lot* of sugar) running around in circles. He has those shoes that light up every time he steps. "Thy word is a lamp to my feet and a light to my path" (Ps 119:105).
- There's a janitor vacuuming the floor and picking up

162 / Ask the Bible Geek®

trash about a hundred feet from me, and no one notices
the work he is humbly putting in. "The greatest among
you is the one who serves" (see Lk 22:27).

- The announcer says that some of the stand-by passen-
gers will make it on the plane. Reminds me of the verse,
"Many are called, but few are chosen" (Mt 22:14).

- There's a couple crying, saying good-bye. Remember, "I
am with you always" (Mt 28:20).

- The people who arrived first, with seats in the front of
the plane, will board last. "The first will be last, and the
last shall be first" (see Mt 19:30).

- I look out the window of the terminal, and the sun is
starting to rise. *The* Son rises (see Lk 24:7).

Look around you, wherever you are sitting right now. *Where* do
you see God? I don't just mean the "easy" answer—like if
you're wearing a cross or have a prayer or verse posted near your
computer. I mean, look around at the world and find God.
He's there.

Finding God in the everyday is a form of prayer—a great
one. God is around you right now, possibly in ways you've
never thought of.

Salvation Given

*But from there you will seek the Lord your God, and you will
find him, if you search after him with all your heart and with
all your soul.*

DEUTERONOMY 4:29

Only a God *so extraordinary* is humble enough to exist in the
ordinary.

Does God Watch Horror Movies?

God "knows what I did every summer," and He must want to "scream."

The eyes of the Lord are in every place, keeping watch on the evil and the good.

PROVERBS 15:3

Situation Explained

Do you think God watches horror movies?

Solution Offered

I love a good horror movie. The problem is that there are so few good ones anymore.

Nowadays it's all these "slasher" flicks with young television actors running around in circles screaming, getting chased, and dying in really gory ways.

That's not suspense. That's not horror. It's not even good moviemaking.

Have you ever watched a horror movie in which the person decides that he or she has to "go investigate" the dark room

164 / ASK THE BIBLE GEEK®

upstairs or the basement, *all alone?*

Do you ever look at the screen and find yourself talking to it? I usually say something like, "No, no, you moron, don't do it. Don't go in there!" Of course, the character can't hear me, so the person does it and ends up dying.

I wondered while watching a horror movie recently (as I shouted at the screen), if that's how it is for God, watching me in my daily life. I wondered if God sits in His (anything but) "Lazy God" recliner, watching my life and saying, "No, BG, don't do that. Don't go down that road. It'll kill you!"

But I, like the moron in the horror movie, think I can *"do it on my own,"* and in my pride I don't listen to God. I can't hear Him, just like the character on screen can't hear me. How many times has God shouted to me when I was putting myself in a spiritually dangerous position, and I refused to listen?

God gives us free will, never forcing Himself or the right decisions on us. That doesn't mean that He doesn't care or doesn't watch. Today's verse reminds us that He *does* watch and *is* watching.

What a great daily reminder for me to choose my paths more carefully.

Salvation Given

The eyes of the Lord are in every place, keeping watch on the evil and the good.

PROVERBS 15:3

So, does God watch horror movies?

My answer: Sometimes God does see horror. It's called our world today.

Is God a Dog-Lover?
Put me on a leash, God—please!

Exhort one another every day,... that none of you may be hard-ened by the deceitfulness of sin ... while it is said, "Today when you hear his voice, do not harden your hearts."

HEBREWS 3:13, 15

Situation Explained

Do you "hear" God's voice? Do you run from it like I do?

Solution Offered

So my dog got out this morning. He got right by me as I closed the door, and he made a break for it, like a prisoner trying to escape over the fence.

I ran down the street, freezing in shorts and a t-shirt, calling out his name, while he continued to run farther and faster. Sometimes he'd stop, let me get close, and even look at me, but once I got *too* close, he'd take off again. It was scary, because I didn't want anything to happen to him, like getting hit by a car or something.

It serves me right, I guess, because he's not the best-trained dog in the world. Heck, he's not even that bright.

Finally I got close enough to get my arms around him and hold him. *No way* was he getting away this time. I carried him all the way home.

It's kind of like you and me with God, huh? Sometimes we run away from God and His voice. The world away from His love and protection is appealing, but no matter how far we run, He doesn't quit. He is *always* calling us back to Him, back into His arms.

When we allow Him to scoop us up and be loved by Him, it sure is nice to be back in His warmth. But that doesn't mean we won't try to "get out" again.

I'm *not* saying that we're like dogs to God, only that just as my dog knows my voice, we know God's voice. Whether or not we choose to listen to it, however, is a very different thing.

A lot of times I don't like to hear what God is telling me in my heart, even though it is what is best for me. Every time I refuse to listen to Him, refuse to turn back to Him, and keep going in my own tracks, I'm risking getting hurt (just like my dog), badly hurt (maybe not in traffic but in some significant way).

It takes true courage to listen for His voice.

As for me, I just need to learn to stop running. I mean, *when* will I learn that I can't outrun Him? He's God. It's not like He can't keep up.

Salvation Given

> *Exhort one another every day,... that none of you may be hardened by the deceitfulness of sin ... while it is said, "Today when you hear his voice, do not harden your hearts."*

> HEBREWS 3:13, 15

I wish I had the love and loyalty for God that my dog has for me. That's my goal.

More About the Bible Geek®

In an effort to help modern-day Christians, especially Catholics, to more frequently read and more easily understand the Sacred Scriptures, the "Bible Geek®" was conceived by Mark Hart and "born" in the late spring of 2000. This book is a compilation of letters written by the Bible Geek® and originally published in email form.

These biweekly email devotionals, known as "Spread the WORD," have been read and shared with hundreds of thousands across the United States and now around the world. The fundamental truths and humor in the Bible Geek® messages have broken through the worldly boundaries of geography, culture, and denomination, finding common ground in Christ.

The Bible Geek® family continues to grow, as each month thousands of new readers subscribe to the free "Spread the WORD" devotionals available through **www.lifeteen.com**. If after reading this book you'd like a practical dose of God's truth delivered directly to your email inbox twice a week, completely free of charge, then stop by the LIFE TEEN website and enter the world of the Bible Geek®.